21 世纪全国高职高专旅游系列规划教材

导游英语

主 编 王 堃

副主编 胡 萍 钱 冷 王桂平

编 委 张斐斐 张培培 解 峰 李云仙

北京大学出版社
PEKING UNIVERSITY PRESS

内容简介

本书系统地介绍我国地理、历史、宗教、古建、民族民俗、饮食、土特名产、旅游资源、中国旅游分区以及旅游礼俗，共有 10 个单元，每个单元包括听力训练、情景对话、阅读理解、应用写作、实训练习和知识链接 6 大部分。本书图文并茂，编排灵活，内容新颖且紧扣行业特点和发展需求，形式多样，从外语学习的角度将听说读写技能与话题有机结合，不仅有情景对话，还有实训项目，在深化导游语言服务技能的基础上突出英语应用能力的培养。

本书适合高等职业技术院校和中等学校旅游相关专业的学生使用，以及旅游行业从业人员的岗前培训。

图书在版编目(CIP)数据

导游英语/王堃主编. —北京：北京大学出版社，2011.8
(21 世纪全国高职高专旅游系列规划教材)
ISBN 978-7-301-18986-3

Ⅰ. ①导… Ⅱ. ①王… Ⅲ. ①导游—英语—高等职业教育—教材 Ⅳ. ①H31

中国版本图书馆 CIP 数据核字(2011)第 105556 号

书　　　　名：	导游英语
著作责任者：	王　堃　主编
策 划 编 辑：	刘国明　李　辉
责 任 编 辑：	刘国明
标 准 书 号：	ISBN 978-7-301-18986-3/H·2853
出　版　者：	北京大学出版社
地　　　　址：	北京市海淀区成府路 205 号　100871
网　　　　址：	http://www.pup.cn　http://www.pup6.com
电　　　　话：	邮购部 62752015　发行部 62750672　编辑部 62750667　出版部 62754962
电 子 邮 箱：	pup_6@163.com
印　刷　者：	三河市富华印装厂
发　行　者：	北京大学出版社
经　销　者：	新华书店
	787 毫米×1092 毫米　16 开本　11.25 印张　261 千字
	2011 年 8 月第 1 版　2011 年 8 月第 1 次印刷
定　　价：	30.00 元(含 1CD)

未经许可，不得以任何方式复制或抄袭本书之部分或全部内容。
版权所有，侵权必究　　举报电话：010-62752024
　　　　　　　　　　　电子邮箱：fd@pup.pku.edu.cn

前　言

当前，我国旅游业的发展处于上升阶段，速度之快超出预想。旅游产业的发展方兴未艾，规模仍存在广大发展空间。旅游专业的发展持续向前，精品和优化仍充满强劲动力。在这样的背景下，"导游英语"作为旅游专业的一门专业核心课程，在旅行社行业、景区行业等领域都是不可或缺的。导游英语属于应用语言范畴，具有明显的职业性和实用性，是(涉外)旅游企业员工在职前和职后必修的一门语言课。因此，编写一本既能体现行业特色又能适合职前教育与在职培训的导游英语教材是很有必要的。

本书从我国的文化入手，从旅游的侧面去挖掘、探索、考证中国文化的博大精深，涉及领域广泛，力求做到点面结合，以面为主，所列文化专题来源于接待旅游团的一线经验，更是外宾很感兴趣也十分想了解的。通过深入浅出、循序渐进地剖析，引领读者进入我国博大精深的历史文化和旅游人文世界。10个单元分别从地理、历史、宗教、古建、民族民俗、饮食、土特名产、旅游资源、中国旅游分区以及旅游礼俗进行叙述，涵盖文化旅游的主要方面。每一章从听、说、读、写等方面巧妙安排话题，体现导游基础知识内容的丰富性和导游应用文体的实用性。

本书具有以下几个特点。

(1) 采用话题教学模式，配置一系列形式活泼的语言能力训练项目，如派对讨论、角色扮演、回答问题等。本着"听说领先"的原则，在着重培养听说能力的同时，每个章节还配有相关的应用文模拟写作训练，旨在为师生提供更多的专业术语和背景知识。

(2) 口语化强，所用语言通俗易懂，内容容易接受记诵。职业教育就是就业教育，就业教育的关键在于将深奥的理论化解为通俗的技术。就学生学习旅游职业语言来说，不在于学到多少深奥的语法结构和华丽修辞，而在于以工作过程的实用性和够用性为原则强化学生的口语表达能力，本书在这方面做了大胆的探索和尝试。

(3) 实用性强，本书所选取的景点介绍是我国旅游资源中的精华，是导游员必备的知识，突出地域特征，具有独特的代表性。结合地方特色，以服务地方旅游经济为基本出发点。

(4) 实训性强，每章的最后一个部分是实训，通过各种形式的语言训练活动提高学生的模拟讲解能力，体现了"教学做合一"和"理实一体化"的高职教育理念。

本书可供各级各类高(中)等教育旅游院校旅游专业学生和教师使用或参考，学完本书共需72学时，建议在一年级上学期起使用，分两个学期或一个学期完成。如有学时不达情况，可以根据使用者所在省市的情况，选择重点章节教学，为学生后续学习当地旅游景点的介绍和考取导游资格证奠定基础。

本书共分10个单元，将导游基础知识和导游实务有机地结合在一起，从听、说、读、写、译等方面培养学生的英语综合运用能力。本书由太原旅游职业学院的王堃担任主编并负责统稿和审阅工作，山东旅游职业学院的胡萍、山东济宁职业学院的钱冷和太原旅游职业学院的王桂平任副主编并承担调研工作。参编人员及各个章节分工如下：王堃(第3单元)，胡萍(第2、10单元)，钱冷(第1、9单元)，王桂平(第6单元)，张斐斐(山东旅游职业学院，第8单元)，张培培(山东旅游职业学院，第7单元)，解峰(太原旅游职业学院，第4单元)，李云仙(太原旅游职业学院，第5单元)。值得一提的是参与编写本书的全体人员均在旅行社和星级饭店挂职顶岗实习，均有企业工作经历，充分体现校企合作。加强校企互动成为本书又一大特色。

本书仅为一家之言，希望读者在使用时能够灵活掌握。由于编者水平有限，加之时间仓促，书中不足之处在所难免，在此恭请旅游界、外语界各位同仁提出意见，以便以后再版时修改。

编　者

2011年3月8日

目 录

Unit 1　Chinese Geography 1
　　Part A　Listening 2
　　Part B　Speaking 3
　　Part C　Reading 6
　　Part D　Writing 11
　　Part E　Practical Training 13

Unit 2　Chinese Culture 15
　　Part A　Listening 16
　　Part B　Speaking 18
　　Part C　Reading 21
　　Part D　Writing 28
　　Part E　Practical Training 29

Unit 3　Chinese Religions 32
　　Part A　Listening 33
　　Part B　Speaking 35
　　Part C　Reading 38
　　Part D　Writing 45
　　Part E　Practical Training 47

Unit 4　Chinese Ancient Architecture 49
　　Part A　Listening 50
　　Part B　Speaking 52
　　Part C　Reading 55
　　Part D　Writing 62
　　Part E　Practical Training 65

Unit 5　Chinese Nationalities and Their Customs 68
　　Part A　Listening 69
　　Part B　Speaking 71
　　Part C　Reading 74

	Part D	Writing	84
	Part E	Practical Training	85

Unit 6 Chinese Cuisine ... 88

	Part A	Listening	89
	Part B	Speaking	91
	Part C	Reading	94
	Part D	Writing	102
	Part E	Practical Training	104

Unit 7 China's Local Specialties ... 107

	Part A	Listening	108
	Part B	Speaking	110
	Part C	Reading	114
	Part D	Writing	120
	Part E	Practical Training	122

Unit 8 Tourism Resources in China ... 125

	Part A	Listening	126
	Part B	Speaking	128
	Part C	Reading	131
	Part D	Writing	135
	Part E	Practical Training	137

Unit 9 Overview of Chinese Tourist Zone Distribution ... 140

	Part A	Listening	141
	Part B	Speaking	143
	Part C	Reading	148
	Part D	Writing	153
	Part E	Practical Training	154

Unit 10 Etiquettes and Customs of China Major Tourist Source Countries and Regions ... 158

	Part A	Listening	159
	Part B	Speaking	161
	Part C	Reading	164
	Part D	Writing	169
	Part E	Practical Training	171

参考文献 ... 174

Chinese Geography

Unit 1

Topic Guidance

There are four coastal waters in China: the Bohai Sea, the Yellow Sea, the East China Sea, and the South China Sea.

China has three geographic regions: mountains to the west; deserts and basins in the northeast; valleys and plains in the east.

Chinese climate is varied: tropical in the south, temperate in the east and cold in the Tibetan Plateau and the northeast.

Warming-up

Read the following questions and discuss with your partner.

1. How much do you know about Chinese Geography?
2. which part do you like in China, mountain, sea or desert? And why?
3. Do you know anything about the Tibetan Plateau?

Look at the following pictures and try to describe it in your own words.

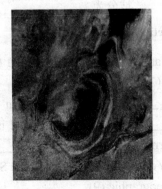

Part A Listening

Words List

population	/ˌpɒpjuˈleɪʃn/	n.	人口；人口数量
civilization	/ˌsɪvəlaɪˈzeɪʃn/	n.	文明；文明社会
nation	/ˈneɪʃn/	n.	国家；民族
crucial	/ˈkruːʃəl/	adj.	至关重要的；关键性的
locate	/ləʊˈkeɪt/	v.	把……安置在(或建造于)
border	/ˈbɔːdə(r)/	n.	国界；边界
region	/ˈriːdʒən/	n.	地区；区域
desert	/ˈdezət/	n.	沙漠；荒漠
basin	/ˈbeɪsn/	n.	盆；盆地；凹地
consist	/kənˈsɪst/	v.	由……组成(或构成)
plateau	/ˈplætəʊ/	n.	高原
Himalayan	/hɪməˈleɪən/	adj.	喜玛拉雅山脉的
Mount Everest	/ˈevərɪst/	n.	珠穆朗玛峰
variation	/ˌveərɪˈeɪʃn/	n.	(数量、水平等)变化，变更
topography	/təˈpɒɡrəfi/	n.	地形；地貌
tropical	/ˈtrɒpɪkl/	adj.	热带的；来自热带的
arid	/ˈærɪd/	adj.	(1) 干旱的；干燥的 (2) 枯燥的；乏味的
temperate	/ˈtempərɪt/	adj.	温带的；温和的

Useful Expressions

in terms of	就……而论；在……方面
based on	以……为基础
play a crucial role	在……中起(至关)重要作用
be divided into	被分为

Activity 1: Spot dictation.

China is the third largest country in the world (1)_____ area but it is the world's largest based on (2)_____.

Chinese (3)_____ began more than 5 000 years ago and the nation has played a (4)_____ role in world history and is (5)_____ to do so today. China is located in Eastern Asia with its (6)_____ along several (7)_____ and the Bohai Sea, the Yellow Sea, the East China Sea, and the South China Sea. China (8)_____ three geographic (9)_____: the (10)_____ to the west, the

Unit 1　Chinese Geography

various (11)_____ and (12)_____ in the northeast and the low lying valleys and (13)_____ in the east. Most of China however (14)_____ mountains and (15)_____ such as the Tibetan Plateau which leads into the Himalayan Mountains and Mount Everest. Because of its area and (16)_____ in (17)_____, China's (18)_____ is also varied. In the south it is (19)_____, while the east is temperate and the Tibetan Plateau is cold and (20)_____. The northern deserts are also arid and the northeast is cold temperate.

Activity 2: Decide whether the following statements are True or False while listening to the paragraph again.

(　　) 1. China plays an important role in the world.

(　　) 2. China is located in Eastern Asia and its climate is cold.

(　　) 3. The Tibetan Plateau leads into the Himalayan Mountains and Mount Everest.

(　　) 4. The climate of Tibetan Plateau is cold and dry.

(　　) 5. China is divided into three geographic regions.

Activity 3: Choose the correct answer while you are listening.

1. How is the China's position in the world in population?
   A. the largest　　　B. the second largest　　C. the third largest
2. What's the population of China?
   A. over 13 billion　　B. over 1.3 million　　C. over 1.3 billion
3. How many bordering countries does China have?
   A. 13　　　　　　　B. 14　　　　　　　　C. 15
4. Whose population is the third in the 56 ethic groups?
   A. Zhuang nationality
   B. Manchu nationality
   C. Hui nationality
5. How many degrees of longitude and latitude does China span?
   A. 49, 62　　　　　B. 62, 49　　　　　　C. 69, 42

Part B　Speaking

Words List

excite	/ikˈsait/	v.	使激动；使兴奋
recognize	/ˈrekəgnaiz/	v.	认出；辨别出；承认
convenient	/kənˈviːniənt/	adj.	便利的；方便的
sightseeing	/ˈsaitsiːiŋ/	n.	游览；观光
reserve	/riˈzəːv/	v.	预订，预约

transportation	/ˌtrænspɔːˈteiʃn/	n.	交通；交通工具
considerate	/kənˈsidərət/	adj.	考虑周到的；体贴的
deluxe	/diˈlʌks/	adj.	豪华的；高级的；奢华的
magnificent	/mægˈnifisnt/	adj.	壮丽的；宏伟的
environmental	/inˌvaiərənˈmentl/	adj.	环境的
nano	/ˈnænəu/	n.	纳米；十亿分之一；毫微
dramatic	/drəˈmætik/	adj.	巨大的；给人印象深刻的；戏剧性的
automobile	/ˈɔːtəməbiːl/	n.	汽车；小轿车
buyout	/ˈbaiaut/	n.	收购；全部买下
dragon	/ˈdrægən/	n.	龙；悍妇

Useful Expressions

equipped with	装备有
prefer to	喜欢
what's more	而且

Proper Nouns

China International Travel Service	中国国际旅行社
Lenovo	联想集团，成立于1984年。公司主要生产台式计算机、服务器、笔记本电脑、打印机、掌上电脑、主机板、手机等电子产品。
IBM	International Business Machines Corporation 国际商业机器公司，或万国商业机器公司的简称。总公司在纽约州阿蒙克市，1911年创立于美国，是全球最大的信息技术和业务解决方案公司，目前拥有全球雇员30多万人，业务遍及160多个国家和地区。
Geely	Geely Automobile Holdings Limited 吉利汽车控股有限公司
Volvo	沃尔沃，瑞典著名汽车品牌，又译为富豪沃尔沃汽车公司，是北欧最大的汽车企业，也是瑞典最大的工业企业集团，世界20大汽车公司之一，创立于1927年。
Standard Bank of South Africa Ltd	南非标准银行。1962年，南非标准银行在南非注册成立，但当时是作为英国标准银行的分支机构在南非运营的。2008年，中国工商银行收购南非标准银行20%股权，成为第一大股东。

Unit 1 Chinese Geography

Benson　　　　　　　　　　　　　　班森(男子名，含义；具有其父般性格的人)
Michael　　　　　　　　　　　　　　(圣经)米迦勒(大天使之一)

Situational dialogue

Miss Li Hua, a local guide from China International Travel Service, is waiting for a business traveler from Australia named Mr. Michael.

L: Hello, sir. Welcome to China! I am Li Hua from China International Travel Service. Nice to meet you.

M: Ah, Nice to meet you Miss Li. I'm Benson Michael. You can call me Benson.

L: Ok. And please call me Li. How's your flight, Benson? I wish it is a wonderful one.

M: Couldn't be better, thanks. I am very excited to come back to China again. China has changed so much that I even cannot recognize since I left here 20 years ago. I wonder if I could stay in a hotel convenient for sightseeing.

L: The hotel you've reserved is only a five minute walk to the business center and quite convenient for transportation.

M: Great! You're really considerate, Li. Thanks a million.

L: You are welcome. I think you need a good rest. Shall we go to the hotel first? This way, please.

(on the way to hotel)

L: How do you feel like here as you come back again after such a long time, Benson?

M: Well, not so wide the road and the building not so high over the past and the city even not so huge, but what a modern city now it is! Everywhere looks deluxe and magnificent.

L: Yeah, we were told these roads and buildings are equipped with the most advanced techniques and the newest environmental friendly materials, say, nano paints, nano air cleaners, nano plastics and other high-techs.

M: Yes, it is a dramatic change in China. We often see commodities made in China now and gradually prefer to use them. Look, my T-shirt also is a Chinese brand named Li Ning.

L: You are right and what's more, Lenovo acquired IBM personal computer, Geely Automobile bought out Volvo and ICBC held Standard Bank of South Africa Ltd. I have to say to be a Chinese, I feel so proud.

M: China is the taking off dragon. And that's why I come to China for business…

L: Well, we are here now. Please go to your room for a short rest. I'll be here at 12:30 and we would like to give you a heart dinner in the Chinese Restaurant. See you around.

Knowledge improvement

With just over 1.3 billion people (1330044605 as of mid-2008; 1338612968 (July 2009)), China is the world's most populous country.

As the world's population is approximately 6.7 billion, China represents a full 20% of the world's population so one in every five people on the planet is a resident of China.

China's population growth has been somewhat slowed by the one child policy, in effect since 1979.

As recently as 1950, China's population was a mere 563 million. The population grew dramatically through the following decades to one billion in the early 1980s.

By the late 2010s, China's population is expected to reach 1.4 billion. China's population is expected to peak in 2026. India will surpass China as the world's most populous country in 2025. Around 2030, China's population is anticipated to peak and then slowly start dropping.

Activity 1: Group discussion.

All the students in the classroom are divided into several groups to discuss what changes do you notice happened in your city, after discussion, each group choose a representative to make a presentation, and then the teacher should give the comment on the students' answer.

Activity 2: Make up a dialogue.

Please practice the dialogue for 5 minutes with your desk mates. After that, the teacher names some students to choose a role to make up a dialogue and then gives comments on their performance if necessary.

Activity 3: Simulated guiding.

All the students in the classroom are divided into several groups, and every group member may try to act as a local guide in class to simulate a situation of introducing a familiar place. Some phrases and expressions you have learnt may be used in your commentary.

Part C   Reading

Words List

officially	/əˈfɪʃəli/	adv.	正式地；官方地
occupy	/ˈɔkjupai/	v.	使用；占用
entire	/inˈtaiə(r)/	adj.	全部的；完全的
approximately	/əˈprɔksimitli/	adv.	大概；近乎
major	/ˈmeidʒə(r)/	adj.	主要的；重要的
surpass	/səˈpɑːs/	v.	超过；胜过；优于
administrative	/ədˈmɪnistrətiv/	adj.	行政的
autonomous	/ɔːˈtɔnəməs/	adj.	自治的；有自治权的

Unit 1 Chinese Geography

municipality	/mjuːˌnisiˈpæliti/	n.	自治市；市政当局
communication	/kəˌmjuːniˈkeiʃn/	n.	(1) 表达；交流；交际 (2) 通信；联络
boundary	/ˈbaundri/	n.	边界；分界线；界限
diverse	/daiˈvəːs/	adj.	相异的；多种多样的
relief	/riˈliːf/	n.	宽慰；轻松；地貌
impenetrable	/imˈpenitrəbl/	adj.	不可进入的；穿不过的
terrain	/təˈrein/	n.	地形；地势
range	/reindʒ/	v.	包括从……到……的各类事物
monsoon	/ˌmɔnˈsuːn/	n.	(1) 雨季；雨季的降雨 (2) 季风；季节风
density	/ˈdensəti/	n.	密集；稠密；密度
strikingly	/ˈstraikiŋli/	adv.	显著地；显目地；突出地
exceptionally	/ikˈsepʃənəli/	adv.	例外地
delta	/ˈdeltə/	n.	(1) 希腊字母表的第 4 个字母 (2) 三角洲
sparsely	/ˈspɑːsli/	adv.	(1) 稀疏地；稀少地 (2) 不足地；贫乏地
barren	/ˈbærən/	adj.	贫瘠的；不毛的
treasury	/ˈtreʒəri/	n.	财政部；国库券
trillion	/ˈtriljən/	n.	万亿；兆
soya	/ˈsɔiə/	n.	大豆
tungsten	/ˈtʌŋstən/	n.	钨
antimony	/ˈæntiməni/	n.	锑
sophisticated	/səˈfistikeitid/	adj.	(1) 老练的；见过世面的 (2) 先进的；精密的
facility	/fəˈsiləti/	n.	设施；设备

Proper Nouns

Tarim	塔里木, 塔里木盆地在新疆南部, 位于天山和昆仑山, 阿尔金山之间, 东西长 1400 千米, 南北宽约 550 千米, 面积达 56 万平方千米, 为我国最大的内陆盆地。
Junggar	准噶尔(蒙古语), 是厄拉特蒙古的一支部落。17 世纪到 18 世纪, 准噶尔部控制天山南北, 在西起巴尔喀什湖, 北越阿尔泰山, 东到吐鲁番, 西南至吹河, 塔拉斯河的广大地区, 建立了史上最后的游牧帝国。在宗教上他们信奉藏传佛教, 对西藏也有一定的影响力。另有准噶尔盆地。
Lop Nur	罗布泊, 是位于中国新疆维吾尔自治区东南部的湖泊。在塔

里木盆地东部，海拔 780 米左右，位于塔里木盆地的最低处。蒙古语罗布泊即多水汇入之湖，古代称为泑泽、盐泽、蒲昌海等，为中国第二大咸水湖，现仅为大片盐壳。

PPP	购买力评价
Treasury securities	国库券
joint venture	合资企业；合营企业
IMF	International Monetary Fund，国际货币基金组织(联合国组织，关注贸易和经济的发展)

Brief Introduction of China

China, officially People's Republic of China, is a country of East Asia. It is the largest of all Asian countries and has the largest population of any country in the world. Occupying nearly the entire East Asian landmass, it occupies approximately one-fourteenth of the land area of the Earth. Among the major countries of the world, China is surpassed in area by only Russia and Canada, and it is almost as large as the whole of Europe.

China has 34 administrative units directly under the central government; these consist of 23 provinces, 5 autonomous regions, 4 municipalities (Chongqing, Beijing, Shanghai, and Tianjin), and 2 special administrative regions (Hong Kong and Macau). Beijing (Peking), the capital of the People's Republic, is also the cultural, economic, and communications centre of the country.

Within China's boundaries exists a highly diverse and complex country. Its topography covers the highest and one of the lowest places on Earth, and its relief varies from nearly impenetrable mountainous terrain to vast coastal lowlands. Its climate ranges from extremely dry, desertlike conditions in the northwest to tropical monsoon in the southeast, and China has the greatest contrast in temperature between its northern and southern borders of any country in the world.

Population Distribution

China's complex natural conditions have produced an unevenly distributed population. Population density varies strikingly, with the greatest contrast occurring between the eastern half of China and the lands of the west and the northwest. Exceptionally high population densities occur in the Yangtze delta, the Pearl River Delta, and on the Chengdu Plain of the western Sichuan Basin.

In contrast, the isolated, extensive western and frontier regions, which are much larger than any European country, are sparsely populated. Extensive uninhabited areas include the extremely high northern part of Tibet, the sandy wastes of the central Tarim and eastern Junggar basins in Xinjiang, and the barren desert and mountains east of Lop Nur.

Unit 1 Chinese Geography

Economy

The People's Republic of China stands as the second-largest economy both in nominal and *purchasing power parity* terms (PPP) in the world after the US. It is the world's fastest-growing major economy, with average growth rates of 10% for the past 30 years. China is the largest creditor nation in the world and owns approximately 20.8% of all foreign-owned US Treasury securities. China is also the largest exporter and second largest importer of goods in the world. Its top six trade partners (US, Japan, Hong Kong, South Korea, Taiwan, Germany) form over 50% of China's total international trade.

For 2010, inbound foreign direct investment into China surpassed $100billion for the first time, and investment overseas by Chinese companies in non-financial sectors totaled $59 billion. But the provinces in the coastal regions of China tend to be more industrialized, while regions in the hinterland are less developed. In the second quarter of 2010, China's economy was valued at $1.33 trillion, ahead of the $1.28 trillion that Japan's economy was worth.

China is the world's largest producer of rice and is among the principal sources of wheat, corn (maize), tobacco, soya beans, peanuts (groundnuts), and cotton. The country is one of the world's largest producers of a number of industrial and mineral products—including cotton cloth, tungsten, and antimony—and is an important producer of cotton yarn, coal, crude oil, and a number of other products. Its mineral resources are probably among the richest in the world. China has acquired some highly sophisticated production facilities through foreign investment and joint ventures with foreign partners. The technological level and quality standards of many of its industries have improved rapidly and dramatically.

The table below shows the trend of the GDP of China at market prices estimated by the IMF with figures in millions (Chinese yuan).

Year	Gross domestic product	US dollar exchange	Inflation index (2000=100)	Per Capita Income (as % of USA)
1955	91000	2.46	19.2	2.43
1960	145700	2.46	20.0	3.04
1965	171600	2.46	21.6	2.63
1970	225300	2.46	21.3	2.20
1975	299700	1.86	22.4	2.32
1980	460906	1.49	25.0	2.52
1985	896440	2.93	30.0	1.65
1990	1854790	4.78	49.0	1.48
1995	6079400	8.35	91.0	2.17
2000	9921500	8.27	100.0	2.69
2005	18308500	8.19	106.0	4.05
2010	25506956	6.67	112.0	6.23

Despite the size, the wealth of its resources, and the fact that about one-fifth of the world's population lives within its borders, China now still is a developing country. Available energy has not been sufficient to run all of the country's installed industrial capacity, the transport system has remained inadequate to move sufficient quantities of such critical commodities as coal, and the communications system has not been able to meet the needs of China's size and complexity. We need devote all ourselves to its thriving.

Activity 1: Choose the correct answer to complete the following sentences.

1. Among the major countries of the world, China is the_____ largest country.
   A. first   B. second   C. third
2. Chinese climate in the northwest is very_____ .
   A. dry   B. tropical   C. wet
3. Extensive uninhabited areas include eastern Junggar basins in Xinjiang and_____.
   A. the Chengdu Plain of the western Sichuan Basin
   B. east of Lop Nur
   C. 5 autonomous regions
4. Which of the following is not true?
   A. the People's Republic of China stands as the second-largest economy.
   B. In the second quarter of 2010, China's economy was ahead of Japan's economy.
   C. Chinese mineral resources are very deficient in the world.
5. In the year 1970, the US dollar exchange is_____ .
   A. 2.46   B. 8.19   C. 4.78

Activity 2: Fill in the blanks with the words given below. Change the form where necessary.

   approximate   occupy   average   distribution   valuable

1. Imperial gardens_____large areas.
2. Last Sunday, we took a long journey and it took _____seven hours.
3. The teacher asks the representative to_____the relative paper to all trainees.
4. The tour guide told us that more than two million stone blocks were used to build Khufu Pyramid (胡夫金字塔), weighing an _____ of 2.5 tons each.
5. I don't agree with you. As I see it, Kobe has carried on the_____of the Jordan.

Activity 3: Answer the following open questions in brief.

1. Do you know how many administrative units there are in China? And which province are you from? What do you know about your province?
2. How do you feel about Chinese rapidly developing?
3. If any foreign country you may go to, which one will you choose? And why?
4. China is rich in natural resources, but not in average. How to deal with it, in your opinion?
5. What can you learn from the table in the text?

Unit 1　Chinese Geography

Part D　Writing

Plan the Tour Schedule

　　工作计划就是对即将开展的工作的设想和安排，如提出任务、指标、完成时间和步骤方法等。有了计划，工作就有了明确的目标和具体的步骤，就可以协调大家的行动，增强工作的主动性，减少盲目性，使工作有条不紊地进行。旅游计划是为一个旅游团队即将在旅游目的地进行的食宿和游览活动等作出的设想和安排，制订此计划时要掌握旅游团的基本情况，如国籍、人数、停留时间；精心设计旅游期间游客的游览活动，如参观景点、购物、会务等；满足旅游者的食宿要求，如饮食禁忌、三餐时间、酒店标准和购物点等。旅游计划是导游员为客人提供服务的依据，使其工作具有具体的目标和定位，按照步骤进行协调，保证旅游团的接待质量。

　　例如：××旅行社大连、旅顺、威海、烟台、蓬莱、青岛5日游出团计划

天数	线路	交通	活动安排	住宿
D1	上海—山东青岛	专车	上海出发乘车赴山东青岛，抵达后，游览青岛新标志五四广场(1h)，远眺2008年奥运帆船赛场。游览海上栈桥(1h)。乘船游大海(0.5h)，车经万国建筑博览八大关风景区，海滨沙滩自由活动(2h)	青岛××酒店(三星级)(含第二日早餐)
D2	青岛—威海—烟台	专车	参观清末北洋水师旗舰定远舰(1h)，外观素有"小布达拉宫"之称的威海市政府，远眺刘公岛。韩国服装城自由活动(2h)。后赴烟台，游靓丽海滨路、月亮湾、海研所(总2h)	晚宿赴大连船上
D3	大连—旅顺	专车	游览旅顺军港公园、电岩炮台、东鸡冠山景区、蛇博物馆(4个景点各0.5h)。途观友谊塔、胜利塔，参观鳄鱼园泰国民俗风情歌舞表演(费用自理，60元，1h)。返回大连，游星海公园、海水浴场自由活动(1.5h)。晚上可自愿欣赏东北特色二人转表演(40～120元自理，2.5h)	大连××国际酒店(四星级)(含第二日早餐)
D4	大连	专车	早乘车途经中山广场等，观老虎滩极地海洋动物馆(门票自理，190元，3.5h)，虎雕广场，途经104号导弹驱逐舰，乘车游山海相依的情人路——滨海路、北大桥(1h)，游览亚洲最大的城市广场——星海湾广场(0.75h)，欣赏大连建市百年标志：城雕，华表。逛俄罗斯风情街(1h)	晚宿赴山东船上
D5	蓬莱	专车	游览蓬莱八仙过海口风景区(1.5h)，主要景点有八仙祠、会仙阁、望瀛楼等。远眺蓬莱阁和黄渤海分界线	返程

备注：1. 晚间活动属个人行为，无车、无导游跟随。

2. 本次旅游中的所有自费项目由旅游者自愿选择参与，旅行社和导游不会强行安排。

3. 退团：旅游者如在出团前 24 小时内退团，旅行社只退还未产生的单项费用，车费、火车票、飞机票等相关费用不退；旅游者在首日发团及旅游全程中，如迟到 10 分钟且联系不上者视作自动退团或离团，由此产生的各项费用由旅游者本人承担。旅行社如在出团前 24 小时内取消旅游计划，应全额退还旅游者所缴纳的旅游费用，并补偿旅游者所缴纳旅游费用的 10%作为违约金。

4. 3 周岁以下儿童不收取任何费用，旅行社也不承担任何连带责任。

Simulated Writing

Directions: According to tips of the following dialogue, please use the words, phrases or expressions you have learnt to make a schedule.

Dialogue

John is a guest who wants to have a trip to Shanghai, Shenzhen and Hong Kong, Mary is a clerk of travel Service in Chengdu. They are talking about a tour plan.

Mary: Good morning, sir. What can I do for you?

John: Hi, I'm planning a trip to Shanghai and Shenzhen, with Hong Kong as a final destination. Would you please make the necessary arrangements for me?

Many: Certainly, sir. How would you like to go?

John: I'd like to go by train from here to Shanghai and spend at least two days there; visiting scenic spots and shopping are my major activities. Then I'd like to fly to Shenzhen for a business meeting of two nights. I want to go on to Hong Kong by plane for an indefinite stay of two or three days.

Mary: I'll get in touch with the railroad and airline passenger representations immediately. Do you still want a bedroom?

John: Yes.

Mary: When do you plan to leave?

John: I expect to depart for shanghai the day after tomorrow, err… that's June 8th, I'll spend the evening of the 9th and all day the 10th there. I'll leave on the 11th, on either a late afternoon or an early evening flight for Shenzhen. I plan to leave for Hong Kong on an early morning flight on the 13th. I want to travel in Hong Kong only by myself. By the way, please book an open return flight from Hong Kong.

Mary: Will you fly first class as usual, sir? And where shall I make hotel reservation?

John: Yes, first class. I've been quite satisfied with the hotels I've used as lodging before in these cites. Please make reservation for me at those places. Get all the information together, and please report back to me as soon as possible.

Unit 1 Chinese Geography

Part E Practical Training

Training item 1: Oral Presentation

Directions: You are required to work with your group members to finish the task in this part. Every group should choose an aspect about China's development you are familiar to give an introduction. After preparation and practice, a group member will be asked to make an oral presentation, and other students may have additional remarks or explanation if necessary.

Training item 2: Role-play

Directions: All the students in the class are divided into several groups, every member in the group choose one role to perform. Students should use the language they have learnt as far as possible.

Situation 1: Ms. Brown, a tourist from USA. A local guide Lily is taking her to the hotel. Lily is giving a brief introduction of China to her.

Situation 2: Lily, a local guide from China International Travel Service, is making a travelling schedule for the tourists from England.

Training item 3: Outside-class Work

Directions: Please find some information about other countries from books, Internet or some other channels. Try to compare and explain some characteristics of them and then make a brief introduction.

Knowledge links

Achievements of China

In history

In more than a millennium from the Qin Dynasty to the Yuan Dynasty, Chinese science and technology took the lead in the world, and contributed greatly to the progress of the human civilization. An English science historian Bernard said, "For many centuries China was one of the great centers of human civilization and science." Another English science historian Joseph Needham pointed out, "In many important respects the Chinese made scientific and technological inventions ahead of the legendary figures who created famous 'hopeful miracles'. Between the third century A.D. and the 13th. Century A.D., the Chinese kept scientific knowledge at a level far above that of the western world."

At present

China enters its lunar new year on Wednesday, February 3, 2011 in anything but rabbit fashion. Having overtaken Japan to become the world's second biggest economy late in 2010, it has just unveiled economic figures that underline its continuing ability to deliver high levels of growth (10.3 per cent) accompanied by a string of superlatives—from having the world's biggest car market (13.8 million sales) to holding the largest cache of foreign reserves ($2.85trn). At this rate it will be the biggest economy by GDP in the world by the end of 2025. But the GDP per person will be relatively low. Currently it's about $4300 per person (around 95th in the world), and in 2025 it will be about $15000 (roughly 40th in the world). Goldman Sachs forecasts that the last major power ruled by a Communist Party will surpass the United States by 2027. Others see this happening earlier.

For many Americans, China's ascendancy appears already to be a fact: though the US economy is well over twice as big as China's, a recent poll of Americans showed 47 per cent naming China as the world's leading economy compared to 31 per cent who opted for their own country. The US magazine Forbes recently named the Chinese leader, Hu Jintao, as the most powerful man on earth.

China has achieved great success over three decades in which more people have been made materially better off in a shorter space of time than ever before in human history. China drives world commodity markets, affecting economies from Angola to Australia. Chinese companies are buying into Sweden's Volvo car firm, power companies in Brazil, dairy farms in New Zealand and an oil refinery in Scotland, while also hoping that Washington will lift national security obstacles to their purchase of US hi-tech outfits. With its rapidly swelling band of very rich people, China has become a magnet for Western luxury goods. It is the biggest market for fine wine from Bordeaux(波尔多酒). Chinese buyers have sent prices for antiques they want to repatriate spiraling up, including £53m for a Qing Dynasty vase found in a London attic. Smart Paris shops ration the number of items they will allow each Chinese tourist to buy. In the US, hotel chains are serving congee porridge(粥) for Chinese breakfast. Away from the economy, the sheer size of China and its population mean that the statistics from China easily take on enormous proportions. It leads the world in cigarette smoking, mobile telephone and internet use.

At a time of uncertainty and turbulence elsewhere, China appears to be a better organized and more rational state of the world.

Chinese Culture

Unit 2

Topic Guidance

There is rich history and culture in China: calligraphy, painting, folk music and literature.

Excellent celebrities of the past ages have made great contribution in China history.

A survey of history and culture in China will show a wonderful picture of China tourism resource.

Warming-up

Read the following questions and discuss with your partner.

1. How much do you know about the celebrities of the past ages in China?

2. Have you ever listened to the folk music? What folk music do you know ?

3. Do you know the Chinese painting and calligraphy? Why are they renowned in home and abroad?

Look at the following pictures and try to describe it in your own words.

Part A Listening

Words List

customs	/ˈkʌstəmz/	n.	风俗
ethnic	/ˈeθnik/	adj.	种族的；人种的
complex	/ˈkɔmpleks/	n.	复合体；综合设施
dominant	/ˈdɔminənt/	adj.	显性的；占优势的；支配的
identity	/aiˈdentəti/	n.	身份；同一性，一致；特性
assimilate	/əˈsiməleit/	v.	吸收；使同化；把……比作
linguistic	/liŋˈgwistik/	adj.	语言的；语言学的
trace	/treis/	n.	痕迹；踪迹
community	/kəˈmju:nəti/	n.	社区；团体；共同体；群落
distinguish	/diˈstiŋgwiʃ/	n.	辨别；区分；使杰出
ancestral	/ænˈsestrəl/	adj.	祖先的；祖传的
represent	/ˌrepriˈzent/	v.	代表；表现；描绘；回忆
proverb	/ˈprɔvə:b/	n.	谚语，格言；众所周知的人或事

Useful Expressions

Be divided into	被分成
give rise to	产生
In general	通常；大体上
Ethnic group	少数民族
Eastern Asia	东亚
Han Chinese	汉族
cultural identity	文化身份
aged ginger	老姜
hickory nut	山核桃
family name	姓氏

Proper Nouns

chenpi	陈皮
Lin'an	临安

Activity 1: Spot dictation.

The (1)_____of China is one of the world's oldest and most (2)_____cultures. The area in which the culture is (3)_____covers a large(4)_____region in eastern Asia with (5)_____varying greatly between towns, cities and provinces. Today there are 56

Unit 2 Chinese Culture

distinct recognized ethnic groups in China. In terms of numbers, however, the (6)_____ ethnic group is the Han Chinese. Throughout history, many groups have been (7)_____ into neighboring ethnicities or disappeared without a (8)_____. At the same time, many within the Han (9)_____ have maintained distinct (10)_____ and regional cultural traditions. The term Zhonghua Minzu has been used to describe the (11)_____ of Chinese (12)_____ in general. Much of the traditional cultural identity within the (13)_____ has to do with (14)_____ the family name.

Traditional Chinese Culture covers large geographical (15)_____, where each region is usually divided into distinct sub-cultures. Each region is often represented by three (16)_____ items. For example Guangdong is (17)_____ by chenpi, aged ginger and (18)_____. Others include ancient cities like Lin'an, which include tea leaf, bamboo shoot trunk and hickory nut. Such distinctions give rise to the old Chinese (19)_____: "十里不同风，百里不同俗", (20)_____ "the wind varies within ten li, customs vary within a hundred li".

Activity 2: Decide whether the following statements are True or False while listening to the paragraph again.

(　　) 1. China is the oldest and most complex culture in the world.

(　　) 2. Han Chinese is the main ethnic group in China.

(　　) 3. Much of the traditional cultural identity within the community has to do with distinguishing the family name.

(　　) 4. The area in which the culture is dominant covers a large region in western Asia with varying greatly between towns, cities and provinces.

(　　) 5. Traditional Chinese culture covers large geographical territories, where only some region is usually divided into distinct sub-cultures.

Activity 3: Choose the correct answer while you are listening.

1. How many ethnic groups are mentioned in the conversation?
   A. 54　　　　　B. 55　　　　　C. 56

2. What does Zhonghua Minzu mean?
   A. It means Chinese philosophy.
   B. It means the main ethnic group.
   C. It is used to describe the notion of Chinese nationalism in general.

3. Why are there varying customs and traditions in China?
   A. Because China covers a large geographical region.
   B. Because China is one of the world's oldest and most complex cultures.
   C. Both A and B.

4. Guangdong is represented by three items, which are Chenpi, ginger and_____?
   A. bamboo　　　　B. hay　　　　C. tea leaves

5. The old Chinese proverb "十里不同风，百里不同俗" means_____
   A. the wind varies within ten li, customs vary within a hundred li".
   B. customs vary within a hundred li.
   C. the wind varies within ten li, and customs vary within a hundred li.

Part B   Speaking

Words List

Latinate	/ˈlætineit/	adj.	从拉丁语派生(或演化)的
version	/ˈvɜːʃn/	n.	说法；描述
renowned	/rɪˈnaʊnd/	adj.	有名的；闻名的；受尊敬的
absolutely	/ˈæbsəluːtli/	adj.	绝对地；完全地
professional	/prəˈfeʃnl/	adj.	职业的；专业的
moral	/ˈmɔrəl/	adj.	道义上的；道德上的
predominant	/prɪˈdɔmɪnənt/	adj.	占优势的；主导的
stimulate	/ˈstɪmjuleɪt/	v.	促进；激发；激励
discourse	/ˈdɪskɔːs/	n.	论文；演讲
classics	/ˈklæsɪks/	n.	古语文;古典文学
ceremony	/ˈserəməni/	n.	典礼；仪式
disciple	/dɪˈsaɪpl/	n.	信徒；门徒；追随者
doctrine	/ˈdɔktrɪn/	n.	教义；主义；学说；信条
benevolence	/bɪˈnevələns/	n.	仁慈；善心；善意
loyalty	/ˈlɔɪəlti/	n.	忠诚；忠实；忠心耿耿
reputation	/ˌrepjuˈteɪʃn/	n.	名誉；名声
reciprocity	/ˌresɪˈprɔsəti/	n.	互惠；互助；互换

Useful Expressions

given name	名字
be honored for	因……而获得的赞誉
approach to education	教育方法
pose questions	提出问题
molding of the personality	塑造人格
in the way of informal conversations	以非正式交流的方式
roughly speaking	大致说来
ducal states	诸侯国
in addition to	除……之外

Unit 2　Chinese Culture

Proper Nouns

Confucianism	儒家学说
Master Kong	孔圣人
Mencius	孟子
the Five Classics	五书
the Four Books	四经
the Yijing (Classic of Changes)	易经
Shujing (Classic of History)	书
Shijing (Classic of Poetry)	诗经
Liji (Classic of Rites)	礼
Chunqiu (The Annals of the Spring and Autumn Period)	春秋
China Shandong International Travel Service	山东国旅

Situational dialogue

Miss Li hua, a local guide from China Shandong International Travel Service, is showing guests from the United States around Confucius Temple, the largest Confucius temple in the world.

T: tourists　　　G: local guide

G: Ladies and gentlemen, now what we are on the way to visit is Confucius Temple. First of all, let me introduce Confucius before experiencing the Confucianism in the great building complex. Confucius was born in 551 B.C. at Qufu in the State of Lu and died in 479 B.C.. His given name was Qiu and courtest name Zhongni. The name "Confucius" is a Latinate version of "Kong Fuzi," meaning "Master Kong". Confucius and Confucianism have been known to the western world only since the late 16th century.

T: Miss Li, I have heard that Confucius is the renowned thinker and teacher of ancient China. Is it right?

G: Yes，absolutely right. Confucius is the first professional teacher that we know of in ancient China. As a great teacher, Confucius was honored for his approach to education. Confucius taught a system of moral wisdom that would become a predominant social force in China.

T: Why was Confucius honored for his approach to education?

G: Because Confucius stimulated his students to think by posing questions and maintained that the molding of the personality was of prime importance in education, and everything followed from this. His teaching style was more in the way of informal conversations than formal classes. Roughly speaking, his discourse covered three fields, the classics and philosophy, including his views on reforms which would bring the government of the ducal states back to what he considered the ideal of ancient times, the forms and ceremonies of those past times, and poetry and music.

T: Why is the philosophy of Confucius called "Confucianism"?

G: In ancient times, a learned man like Confucius was called *Ru* or *scholar*. That is why the school of thought developed by Confucius was called " Ruxue" in Chinese, which traditionally has been translated into English as Confucianism.

T: There're 72 disciples who were the brightest and spent the most time with him, aren't there?

G: Yes. Altogether at one time or another some 3000 young men came to study un confuciusly. 72 disciples were well known in history. Some of them went with his travels to other states. Major interpreters of Confucian doctrine have included Mencius (Mengzi, 4th cent. B.C.) and Xunzi (3rd cent. B.C.).

T: What a great teacher!

G: Ladies and gentlemen, the central doctrine of Confucianism is ren, which means goodness, benevolence, humanity and kind-heartedness. Related teachings include loyalty, respect and consideration, propriety, reciprocity, neighborliness and love.

G: In addition to teaching, what did Confucius do in his life?

T: A good question. In spite of Confucius abilities and his reputation for wisdom、Confucius had difficulty in finding a suitable position in government and receiving little attention to realize his dream. After he had served the government in some minor positions and in between he found rare opportunities to give political advice and nowhere did he receive much attention. As Confucius' learning and wisdom increased, he began to attract students and disciples. It was when he reached fifty years old that Confucius recognized his divine mission. Besides teaching, Confucius spent much of his last years writing and emending a number of books. The Confucianism is contained in the nine ancient works: the Five Classics and the Four Books. The Five Classics, which originated before the time of by Confucius are the Yijing (Classic of Changes), Shujing (Classic of History), Shijing(Classic of Poetry), Liji(Classic of Rites) , and Chunqiu (The Annals of the Spring and Autumn Period). The only work that Confucius brought out is the Annals of the Spring and Autumn Period, the first historical work in Chinese history.

T: Oh, I see. That sounds interesting.

Knowledge Improvement

Wang Xizhi was a famous calligrapher, traditionally referred to as the Sage of Calligraphy , who lived during the Jin Dynasty (265—420). He is considered by many to be one of the most esteemed Chinese calligraphers of all time, especially during and after the Tang Dynasty, and a master of all forms of Chinese calligraphy, especially the running script.Born in Linyi, Shandong, Wang spent most of his life in present-day Shaoxing, Zhejiang. He learned the art of calligraphy from Lady Wei Shuo. He excelled in every script but particularly in semi-cursive script. His most famous work is the Preface to the Poems

Unit 2 Chinese Culture

Composed at the Orchid Pavilion, the introduction to a collection of poems written by a number of poets during a gathering at Lanting near the town of Shaoxing for the Spring Purification Festival. The original is lost, but there are a number of finely traced copies and rubbings in existence.

Activity 1: Group discussion.

All the students in the classroom are divided into several groups to discuss what important information about Confucius is mentioned in the dialogue, after discussion, each group choose a representative to make a presentation, and then the teacher should gives the comments on students' answer.

Activity 2: Make up a dialogue.

Please practice the dialogue for 5 minutes with your deskmates. After that, teacher names some students to choose a role to make up a dialogue and then give comments on their performance if necessary.

Activity 3: Simulated guiding.

All the students in the classroom are divided into several groups, and every group member may try to act as a local guide in class to simulate a situation of introducing a celebrity. Some phrases and expressions you have learnt may be used in your commentary.

Part C Reading

Word List

calligraphy	/kəˈlɪgrəfi/	n.	书法；书法艺术
visual	/ˈvɪʒuəl/	adj.	视力的；视觉的
harmonious	/hɑːˈməʊniəs/	adj.	友好和睦的；和谐的
aesthetic	/iːsˈθetɪk/	adj.	审美的；美学的
evolution	/ˌiːvəˈluːʃn/	n.	演变；发展；渐进
oriental	/ˌɔːriˈentl/	adj.	东方(尤指中国和日本)的
convey	/kənˈveɪ/	v.	表达；传递(思想、感情等)
dynamism	/ˈdaɪnəmɪzəm/	n.	精力；活力；劲头
cognizance	/ˈkɒgnɪzəns/	n.	认识；获知；领悟
intimate	/ˈɪntɪmət/	n.	亲密的；密切的
appeal	/əˈpiːl/	n.	吸引力；感染力；魅力
exaggeration	/ɪgˌzædʒəˈreɪʃn/	n.	夸张；夸大；言过其实
gem	/dʒem/	v.	(经切割打磨的)宝石
pigment	/ˈpɪgmənt/	n.	颜料
lacquer	/ˈlækə(r)/	n.	漆

canvas	/ˈkænvəs/	n.	(帆布)画布；油画
concrete	/ˈkɔŋkriːt/	n.	混凝土
manifest	/ˈmænifest/	v.	表明；清楚显示
photographic	/ˌfəutəˈɡræfik/	adj.	摄影的；摄制的；照片的
composition	/ˌkɔmpəˈziʃn/	n.	成分；构成；组合方式
naturalistic	/ˌnætʃrəˈlistik/	adj.	写实的；顺从自然的
ornamental	/ˌɔːnəˈmentl/	adj.	装饰性的；点缀的
abstraction	/æbˈstrækʃn/	n.	抽象概念；抽象
spiral	/ˈspairəl/	n.	螺旋形；螺旋式
zigzag	/ˈzigzæɡ/	n.	锯齿形线条(形状)；之字形
mount	/maunt/	v.	镶嵌；安置
motif	/məuˈtiːf/	n.	(文学、艺术作品的)主题；中心思想
album	/ˈælbəm/	n.	相册；影集；集邮簿
inhabit	/inˈhæbit/	v.	居住在；栖居于
dominate	/ˈdɔmineit/	n.	支配；控制；左右；影响
juxtaposition	/ˌdʒʌkstəpəˈziʃən/	n.	并置；并列
enshrine	/inˈʃrain/	v.	入庙祀奉
inextricably	/ˌinikˈstrikəbli/	adj.	不可分开地；密不可分地
mythological	/ˌmiθəˈlɔdʒikl/	adj.	神话的；神话学的

Useful Expressions

Visual art	视觉艺术
Chinese characters	汉字
a unique Oriental art	独一无二的东方艺术
be rich in content	内容丰富
moral integrity	诚实
the beauty of image in painting	绘画形象美
the beauty of dynamism in dance	舞蹈动感美
the beauty of rhythm in music	音乐节奏美
belong to	属于
apply to	应用
in nature	本质上
consisted of	包括
rather than	而不是
be mounted on scrolls	在卷轴上裱画
human figure	肖像
as opposed to	与……相反
at the dawn of	在……来临之际
emerging into	融入
in view of	考虑到

Unit 2 Chinese Culture

have little bearing on	对……作用很小
be responsible for	对……负责
in favor of	支持
in response to	作为回答
Music geners	音乐体裁
in the spoken vernacular	用地方方言

Proper Nouns

Five Dynasties period	五代时期
Meticulous – Gong-bi	工笔
Freehand – Shui-mo	水墨
The Sistine Chapel	西斯廷教堂
modern imagist school	现代意象派
the Ming era	明朝

Chinese Culture

Chinese Calligraphy

Calligraphy is a type of visual art. It is often called the art of fancy lettering. A contemporary definition of calligraphic practice is "the art of giving form to signs in an expressive, harmonious and skillful manner". The story of writing is one of aesthetic evolution framed within the technical skills, transmission speed(s) and material limitations of a person, time and place. A style of writing is described as a script, hand or alphabet.

Chinese calligraphy is not only a practical technique for writing Chinese characters, but also a unique Oriental art of expression and a branch of learning or discipline as well. As a branch of learning it is rich in content, including the evolution of writing styles, development and rules of technique, history of calligraphy, calligraphers and their inheritance in art, and evaluation of calligraphy as a work of art. This branch of learning is wide ranging and deep, forming an important part of Chinese culture.

It is very much like painting which uses Chinese characters to communicate the spiritual world of the artist. Through the medium of form, way of handling the brush, presentation and style, calligraphy as a work of art conveys the moral integrity, character, emotions, esthetic feelings and culture of the artist to readers affecting them by the power of appeal and the joy of beauty.

Western scholars praise this form of Chinese art as having the beauty of image in painting, the beauty of dynamism in dance and the beauty of rhythm in music. Thus abstract art—the ultramodern art of the West-takes cognizance of the most ancient art-calligraphy of the East, establishing an intimate relationship between the two. Although calligraphy's home is China, it does not belong exclusively to China. It does not belong exclusively to the East, either. It's no exaggeration to say that calligraphy is a gem in the world's art treasure.

Chinese Painting

Painting is the practice of applying paint, pigment, color or other medium to a surface (support base). The application of the medium is commonly applied to the base with a brush but other objects may be used. In art the term describes both the act and the result which is called a painting. Paintings may have for their support such surfaces as walls, paper, canvas, wood, glass, lacquer, clay, copper or concrete, and may incorporate multiple other materials including sand, clay, paper, gold leaf as well as objects.

Painting is a mode of expression and the forms are numerous. Drawing, composition or abstraction and other aesthetics may serve to manifest the expressive and conceptual intention of the practitioner. Paintings can be naturalistic and representational (as in a still life or landscape painting), photographic, abstract, be loaded with narrative content, symbolism, emotion or be political in nature.

Chinese painting is one of the oldest continuous artistic traditions in the world. The earliest paintings were not representational but ornamental, they consisted of patterns or designs rather than pictures. Early pottery was painted with spirals, zigzags, dots or animals. It was only during the Warring States Period (403—221 B.C.) that artists began to represent the world around them.

Painting in the traditional style is known today in Chinese as guó huà, meaning "national" or "native painting", as opposed to Western styles of art which became popular in China in the 20th century. Traditional painting involves essentially the same techniques as calligraphy and is done with a brush dipped in black or colored ink, oils are not used. As with calligraphy, the most popular materials on which paintings are made of are paper and silk. The finished work is then mounted on scrolls, which can be hung or rolled up. Traditional painting also is done in albums and on walls, lacquerwork and other media.

The two main techniques in Chinese painting are: Meticulous—Gong-bi often referred to as "court-style" painting. Freehand—Shui-mo loosely termed watercolor or brush painting. The Chinese character "mo" means ink and "shui" means water. This style is also referred to as "xie yi" or freehand style.

Artists from the Han (202 B.C.) to the Tang (618—906) Dynasties mainly painted the human figure. Much of what we know of early Chinese figure painting comes from burial sites, where paintings were preserved on silk banners, lacquered objects and tomb walls. Many early tomb paintings were meant to protect the dead or help their souls get to paradise. Others illustrated the teachings of the Chinese philosopher Confucius or showed scenes of daily life.

Many critics consider landscape to be the highest form of Chinese painting. The time from the Five Dynasties period to the Northern Song period (907—1127) is known as the "Great age of Chinese landscape". In the north, artists such as Jing Hao, Fan Kuan and Guo Xi painted pictures of towering mountains, using strong black lines, ink wash and sharp,

Unit 2 Chinese Culture

dotted brushstrokes to suggest rough stone. In the south, Dong Yuan, and other artists painted the rolling hills and rivers of their native countryside in peaceful scenes done with softer, rubbed brushwork. These two kinds of scenes and techniques became the classical styles of Chinese landscape painting.

A portion of the history of painting in both Eastern and Western art is dominated by spiritual motifs and ideas; examples of this kind of painting range from artwork depicting mythological figures on pottery to Biblical scenes rendered on the interior walls and ceiling of The Sistine Chapel, to scenes from the life of Buddha or other scenes of eastern religious origin.

Chinese music

Chinese music started at the dawn of Chinese civilization with documents and artifacts providing evidence of a well-developed musical culture as early as the Zhou Dynasty (1122 B.C.—256 B.C.). As China covers a vast area inhabited by many culturally distinct ethnic groups which have interacted to varying degrees for more than 4000 years; Chinese musical genres are thus numerous and their styles varied. But throughout Chinese musical history a number of central themes dominate a belief in the power of music, necessitating its control by the state; the juxtaposition of "native" and "foreign" (especially central Asian) idioms; and a fascination with theory, acoustics and metaphysical relation of music to the natural world, ideas which are enshrined in hundreds of treatises from the ancient to modern period. Today, the music continues a rich traditional heritage in one aspect, while emerging into a more contemporary form at the same time.

Little is known about the sound of ancient Chinese music, but written documents provide information about music theory and music in society. Chinese musical history has been inextricably bound to politics. The bureau of music of each new administration established pitch standards and oversaw ceremonial and court music. Absolute pitch was regarded as an integral part of the system of weights and measures and new measurements were introduced with each new dynasty. Chinese philosophers (including Confucius) were early to recognize the power of music over the mind and emotions and its importance in education. Like the ancient Greeks, they recommended state control in view of its power over the morality of the masses. Although ancient music theory has little bearing on modern Chinese music these fundamental views have persisted and can be witnessed in such movements as the Cultural Revolution.

From the time Confucianism became the state religion of China in the Han dynasty until the 1911 revolution, yayue ("elegant music", associated with Confucian ritual) was the state music; every dynasty tried to retain its ancient style. After the disappearance of the imperial courts in China, however, yayue has been performed only in Confucian temples. There are over 300 forms of regional theatres in China, the most famous of which is Beijing (Peking) opera. There are four basic types: the main male characters, including bearded old men, court officials and generals (all usually in the baritone range); unbearded scholar-lovers who sing in falsetto; the virtuous daughter or faithful wife, sung in high falsetto; and the flirtatious woman.

Chinese literature

It is not known when the current system of writing Chinese first developed. The oldest written records date from about 1400 B.C. in the period of the Shang Dynasty, but the elaborate system of notation used even then argues in favor of an earlier origin. From short inscriptions on bone and tortoiseshell (used for divination), characters standing for individual words have been deciphered and are traceable through many notations to modern forms.

The early Chinese books originally appeared in the cumbersome form of strips of bamboo. Silk was substituted as a writing material in the 2nd cent B.C., and the invention of paper in the 2nd cent A.D. was responsible for a great increase in the number of books. The method of printing whole pages from wooden blocks was discovered under the Tang Dynasty (618—906) and was perfected and in widespread use by the 10th cent. This technology permitted an enormous increase in the number of copies available of any book.

Over time, the nature of the language in which the literature of China was written diverged sharply, exceedingly concise and unmatched for its vigor, richness and symmetry. Historical and literary allusions abounded, and finally special dictionaries were required for their elucidation. There are two main styles of writing, one composed in a specifically literary language and the other in the vernacular. Both strands produced their own very different styles of literature, and both styles reflected their own characteristic language.

Tang and Song poetry strongly influenced the modern imagist school. Chinese lyrics are generally very short, unemphatic and quiet in manner, and limited to suggesting a mood or a scene by a few touches rather than painting a detailed picture. Intellectual themes and narratives are comparatively rare.

Chinese lexicography developed in response to multiplication of characters. The last of a great series of dictionaries (still in standard use) was produced in the reign of Kangxi emperor (1662—1722). So-called encyclopedias, actually extracts from existing works, have been occasionally compiled.

While the literati were cultivating polite literature during the Tang and Song periods, prose and verse of a popular nature began to appear. It was written in the spoken vernacular rather than in the classical literary language, and scholars regarded it with scorn. Springing from story cycles made familiar by professional storytellers, this vernacular literature first emerged as a full-fledged art in the drama of the Yuan Dynasty.

The vernacular style later developed into the great novels of the Ming period that followed. Both the drama and the novel proved immensely popular. Thus in 13th century, the living language of the common people emerged in literature. The vernacular novels, although they had their roots in the Yuan epoch, took shape gradually during the Ming era

Unit 2 Chinese Culture

until they were finally given their finished form, perhaps anonymously by some talented traditional scholar.

After the republican revolution (1911) authors turned away from the classical modes of composition, and many writers (notably Hu Shi and Lu Xun) advocated writing in the baihua vernacular. In more modern times, the author Lu Xun (1881—1936) is considered the founder of baihua literature in China.

Translations of Western books frequently appeared in China, and the novelists of the republican period were greatly influenced by European writers.

Activity 1: Choose the correct answer to complete the following sentences.

1. Calligraphy is a type of_____art.
   A. visual   B. audio   C. fancy

2. As a branch of learning it is rich in content, including_____, history of calligraphy, calligraphers and their inheritance in art, and evaluation of calligraphy as a work of art.
   A. evolution of writing styles
   B. development and rules of technique
   C. Both A and B

3. The earliest paintings consisted of patterns or designs rather than_____.
   A. stories   B. pictures   C. characters

4. There are_____main techniques in Chinese painting.
   A. 2   B. 3   C. 4

5. Chinese musical history has been inextricably bound to_____.
   A. literature   B. politics   C. economy

Activity 2: Fill in the table according to what you have learnt.

China Culture	Features	Style	Influence
Calligraphy			
Painting			
Music			
Literature			

Activity 3: Answer the following open questions in brief.

1. Do you know any famous painter/calligrapher/musician/writer in China? Who are they?
2. What features do Chinese painting have?
3. What do you know about the modern music?
4. What do you know about oral literature?
5. What can you learn from the culture of China?

导游英语

Part D   Writing

Notice Board

告示就是以书面的形式通知有关人员，告知活动安排等事项，让有关人员知晓。有各种不同形式，常见形式包括通知招领启事、布告、更正、接站牌等。格式安排如下。

(1) 一般在正文上部中间注明招领启事、布告、更正、接站等标题。

(2) 标题下方为通知内容，力求简洁明了，措辞确切。

(3) 发出通知的单位在正文下面略偏右。

(4) 发通知时间既可写在左下角，略低于发通知方，也可写在右下角，发通知方下面。有时时间可以省略。

(5) 旅行社、饭店制作接机牌等通知对象为游客时，通知的称呼写在正文前面，即：Dear Mr/Mrs. 或 Dear Mrs，字面简洁醒目，只要写出最主要的几个字即可，一般是团队领队的名称、标志、徽章或客人的名字。车头纸标明团队的名称或用其标志、徽章即可。空间有限，只在接机牌上写一个人的名字，其他的省略。手写时，一定要书写规范工整、字迹清楚、易于辨认，突出客人的名字；复印的团队名称应显得严肃正规，字号尽可能粗大些，这样有助于迅速找到团队。

Sample 1

通　知

原定于6月10日参观山东省博物馆，现延期，参观日期另行通知。

山东国旅
2010年6月2日

Notice

The visit to Shandong Museum orinially scheduled for 10th June, is now put off until further notice.

CITS Shandong Branch
2nd, June, 2010

Sample 2

制作接机牌

北京中旅 China Travel Service Qingdao Branch 明天去机场接机，团队来自加拿大 Canada Maple Travel Agency，领队 John Smith，请做好接机牌。

Unit 2 Chinese Culture

> Welcome **David Smith** of Canada
> Flight: **CA 151**
> **Toronto – Beijing**
> Reception of **CTS Beijing**

Simulated Writing

Directions: Please use the words, phrases or expressions you have learnt to write a notice / Placard and Sign Boards according to the Chinese tips.

(1) 通知：我们将于2011年2月26日迁到更方便的地方办公：济南经十东路2245号
山东旅游公司
2010年12月28日

(2) 旅去机场接团，团队号BY20110221，领队Chuck Hilton，洛杉矶直飞北京的航班CA423，上午11点降落，请制作接站牌。

Part E   Practical Training

Training item 1: Oral Presentation

Directions: You are required to work with your group members to finish the task in this part. Every group should choose a kind of culture you are familiar to give an introduction. After preparation and practice, a group member will be asked to make an oral presentation; other students may have additional remarks or explanation if necessary. And then the teacher gives comments on the students' performance.

Training item 2: Role-play

Directions: All the students in the class are divided into several groups, every member in the group choose one role to perform. Students should use the language they have learnt as far as possible.

Situation 1: Ms. Brown, a tourist from USA, comes to Shandong province. A local guide Lily is showing her around Mt.Tai——a very famous Mountain in China. Lily is introducing the knowledge of Chinese Calligraphy like the origin, calligrapher, features and the worship between the words, etc.

Situation 2: Ms. Brown is very interested in Painting, and a local guide Lily is giving her brief introduction of Painting. In addition, Lily offers her more knowledge about the difference between Chinese and western painting.

Situation 3: Lily, a local guide from China Shandong International Travel Service, is preparing placard and sign boards for tourists from USA with meeting service at the airport.

Training item 3: Outside-class Work

Directions: Please find some information about other forms of culture in China from books, Internet or some other channels. Try to compare and explain some characteristics of them and then make a brief introduction.

Knowledge links

The Oldest Known Paintings In the World

The oldest known paintings are at the Grotte Chauvet in France, claimed by some historians to be about 32000 years old. They are engraved and painted using red ochre and black pigment and show horses, rhinoceros, lions, buffalo, mammoth or humans often hunting. However the earliest evidence of painting has been discovered in two rock-shelters in Arnhem Land, in northern Australia. In the lowest layer of material at these sites there are used pieces of ochre estimated to be 60000 years old. Archaeologists have also found a fragment of rock painting preserved in a limestone rock-shelter in the Kimberley region of North-Western Australia, that is dated 40000 years old. There are examples of cave paintings all over the world—in France, Spain, Portugal, China, Australia, India etc.

In Western cultures oil painting and watercolor painting have rich and complex in style and subject matter. In the East, ink and color ink historically predominated the choice of media with equally rich and complex traditions.

Four Treasures of the Study

Writing Brush

The earliest writing brush that has been found is a relic of the Warring States Period (476 B.C.—221 B.C.). From that time onwards, the brush has evolved into many forms. It is important to see that there can be both soft and hard brushes each producing their own particular styles. The delicacy gives literators and painters inspiration for creation, and has led to brush shafts being decorated with artistic patterns.

Ink Stick

A good ink stick should be ground so as to be refined black with luster. With the invention of paper, they were improved accordingly. Since the Han Dynasty (206 B.C.—220 B.C.), ink sticks have been made from pine soot, using other procedures that include mixing with glue, steaming and molding. In ancient times, emperors such as Qianlong in the Qing Dynasty (1644—1911) had paid great attention to the production of ink stickes and were expert in their appreciation of quality inks.

Paper

Paper making is among the "four great inventions" and one of the great contribuions that ancient Chinese people made to the world. Before the existence of paper, our ancestors utilized knots in cords to record events. They then carved on bone, ivory, tortoise shell and bronzes. For very many years they wrote on pieces of bamboom. It was Cai Lun who made the valuable contribution and his research gave rise to paper. Afterwards, many varieties of paper were produced of different quality and usage. Today the Xuan paper originally made in Anhui province still shines with its charm.

Ink Slab

The ink slab is the reputed head of the "four treasures", for its sobriety and elegance has endured the passage of time. Through ink slabs, people can sample the artistic charm of sculpting and the ink stone's natural tints. Nearly all Chinese calligraphy enthusiasts hold that the star of ink slab is the Duanyan, ink slab produced in Duanzhou of Guangdong province. It has its base a purple hue and enjoys the poetic name "purple clouds". It was always a tribute to the royal families during the Tang Dynasty (618—907).

Performers and Roles in Beijing Opera

Sheng

The Sheng (生) is the main male role in Beijing opera. This role has numerous subtypes. The laosheng is a dignified older role. These characters have a gentle and cultivated disposition and wear sensible costumes. Young male characters are known as xiaosheng.

Dan

The Dan (旦) refers to any female role in Beijing opera. Dan roles were originally divided into five subtypes. Old women were played by laodan, martial women were wudan, young female warriors were daomadan, virtuous and elite women were qingyi, and vivacious and unmarried women were huadan.

Jing

The Jing (净) is a painted face male role. Depending on the repertoire of the particular troupe, he will play either primary or secondary roles. This type of role will entail a forceful character, so a Jing must have a strong voice and be able to exaggerate gestures.

Chou

The Chou (丑) is a male clown role. The Chou usually plays secondary roles in a troupe. Indeed, most studies of Beijing opera classify the Chou as a minor role. The name of the role is a homophone of the Mandarin Chinese word chou, meaning "ugly". This reflects the traditional belief that the clown's combination of ugliness and laughter could drive away evil spirits. Chou roles can be divided into Wen Chou, civilian roles such as merchants and jailers, and Wu Chou, minor military roles.

Chinese Religions

Unit 3

Topic Guidance

There are three major religions in China: Buddhism, Christianity and Islam.

Chinese people enjoy the freedom to believe or not believe in religion.

All the religious activities can be put into practice in temples, churches and mosques, which are protected by the Chinese government and supervised by the Bureau of Religious Affairs.

Warming-up

Read the following questions and discuss with your partner.

1. How much do you know about the Buddhism?
2. Have you ever read the Bible? What stories do you know from the sacred book?
3. Do you know the festivals of Islam? How do Muslims celebrate?

Look at the following pictures and try to describe it in your own words.

Unit 3 Chinese Religions

Part A Listening

Words List

religion	/rɪˈlɪdʒən/	n.	宗教；宗教信仰
philosophy	/fəˈlɒsəfi/	n.	哲学；哲学体系
system	/ˈsɪstəm/	n.	体系；制度
originate	/əˈrɪdʒɪneɪt/	v.	发源；起源
influence	/ˈɪnfluəns/	n.	影响；作用
policy	/ˈpɒləsi/	n.	政策；方针
issue	/ˈɪʃuː/	n.	问题；争议
constitution	/ˌkɒnstɪˈtjuːʃn/	n.	宪法；章程
harmoniously	/hɑːˈməʊniəsli/	adv.	和谐地；协调地
dispute	/dɪˈspjuːt/	n.	争端；纠纷
atmosphere	/ˈætməsfɪə(r)/	n.	气氛；氛围
spirit	/ˈspɪrɪt/	n.	精神；心灵
tolerance	/ˈtɒlərəns/	n.	宽容；忍受

Useful Expressions

play an important role in	扮演着重要的角色
in addition	此外
have influence on	对……有影响
from generation to generation	一代又一代
in existence	存在
draw up	设立
carry out	实施
in accordance with	按照
multi-religious country	多宗教的国家
politics-religion relationship	政教关系

Proper Nouns

Buddhism	佛教
Christianity	基督教
Islam	伊斯兰教
Confucianism	儒家思想
Confucius	孔子

Activity 1: Spot dictation.

China is a (1)_____ with more than 100 million (2)_____. The main religions in China are (3)_____, which play an _____ (4)_____ history of Chinese culture. In addition, the Confucianism, a kind of ancient (5)_____ and a major (6)_____ that created by Confucius and originated in China, also (7)_____ Chinese people from generation to generation.

In China, respecting and protecting (8)_____ is a long-term (9)_____ of Chinese government for the (10)_____. As a right of citizens, (11)_____ has been protecting by Chinese constitution and law. (12)_____ usually carried in the (13)_____, which are supported by Chinese government. All religions in China (14)_____ and being in existence (15)_____ without any religious disputes. Religious believers and non-believers respect each other, forming the atmosphere of (16)_____. These reflect traditional Chinese (17)_____ and the (18)_____ relationship after the (19)_____ of People's Repudlic of china, current national conditions (20)_____.

Activity 2: Decide whether the following statements are True or False while listening to the paragraph again.

(   ) 1. People can believe in a religion freely in China.

(   ) 2. The Confucius is a major system of thought that have influenced on Chinese people for a long time.

(   ) 3. All religions in China are equal and existed with harmony.

(   ) 4. The religious activities are protected by Chinese law.

(   ) 5. Respecting and protecting religious freedom is not a long-term basic national policy.

Activity 3: Choose the correct answer while you are listening.

1. How many kinds of religions are mentioned in the conversation?
   A. 2   B. 3   C. 4

2. What does the man mean?
   A. The Confucianism is Chinese philosophy.
   B. The Confucianism is Chinese book.
   C. The Confucianism is Chinese policy.

3. Why do most Chinese people usually believe in Buddhism?
   A. Buddhism was significant to Chinese people.
   B. Buddhism was introduced into China firstly.
   C. Buddhism was originated in China.

Unit 3 Chinese Religions

4. Which religion is related to Christmas?
   A. Buddhism
   B. Islam
   C. Christianity
5. When was Islam introduced in China?
   A. Eastern Han Dynasty
   B. Tang Dynasty
   C. Song Dynasty

Part B Speaking

Words List

profoundity	/prəˈfʌnditi/	n.	博大精深
absolutely	/ˈæbsəluːtli/	adv.	绝对地；完全地
vicissitude	/viˈsisitjuːd/	n.	变迁；盛衰
ruin	/ˈruːin/	n.	毁灭；破坏
eminent	/ˈeminənt/	adj.	卓越的；著名的
bundle	/ˈbʌndl/	n.	捆；包
sutra	/ˈsuːtrə/	n.	佛经
distribute	/diˈstribjuːt/	v.	分散；分布
decorate	/ˈdekəreit/	v.	装饰；装潢
respectively	/riˈspektivli/	adv.	各自地；分别地
symbolize	/ˈsimbəlaiz/	v.	象征；代表
model	/ˈmɒdl/	v.	制作模型
artistic	/ɑːˈtistik/	adj	艺术的；精美的
prominent	/ˈprɒminənt/	adj.	重要的；杰出的
tiered	/tiəd/	adj.	分层的；成排的
amazing	/əˈmeiziŋ/	adj.	令人惊奇的
splendid	/ˈsplendid/	adj.	豪华的；雄伟的

Useful Expressions

be honored as	被评为
north-south central axis	南北中轴线
in charge of	负责，掌管
be deeply impressed by	被深深打动
originating court	祖庭

Proper Nouns

China Henan International Travel Service	中国河南国际旅行社
White Horse Temple	白马寺
Jiashi Moteng	迦什摩腾
Zhu Falan	竺法兰
the Heavenly King Hall	天王殿
the Great Buddha Hall	大佛殿
the Daxiong Hall	大雄宝殿
the Jieyin Hall	接引殿
Qingliang Terrace	清凉台
Pilu Pavilion	毗卢阁
Sakyamuni Buddha	释迦牟尼佛
Manjusri	文殊菩萨
Samantabhadra	普贤菩萨
Medicine Buddha	药师佛
Amitabha Buddha	阿弥陀佛

Situational dialogue

Miss Li hua, a local guide from China Henan International Travel Service, is showing guests from New Zealand around a famous Buddhist holy site—White Horse Temple, the first Buddhist temple in China.

T: tourists   G: local guide

G: Ladies and gentlemen, now what we are going to visit is a very famous Buddhist temple which is called White Horse Temple. Follow me, please, let's experience the profundity of Buddhism.

T: Miss Li, I have heard that this temple is the first Buddhist temple in China. Is it right?

G: Yes, absolutely right. The White Horse Temple is honored as the "Cradle of Buddhism in China" and known as the "originating court" of Chinese Buddhism.

T: When was it built?

G: It was established in the 11th year (68 A.D.) during the Yongping reign of Emperor Mingdi in the Eastern Han Dynasty (25—220) and has a history of over 1900 years. The White Horse Temple has experienced vicissitudes and ruin in ancient times, it was rebuilt several times.

T: Then why is it called the "White Horse Temple"?

G: All right, good question. Here is an interesting legend related to the temple. It is said that Emperor Mingdi of the Eastern Han dreamed of a golden figure flying over his palace. The emperor told his ministers about the dream, and they suggested the figure might be the

Unit 3 Chinese Religions

Buddha in India. Several people were thus sent to India to learn more about Buddhism. After three years, they returned with two eminent Indian monks, Jiashi Moteng and Zhu Falan. The monks brought with them a white horse carrying a bundle of Buddhist sutras and figures. The next year, the emperor ordered the construction of a temple named White Horse Temple to honor the arrival of Buddhism in China and the horse that carried back the sutras.

T: Oh, I see. That sounds interesting. Let's see it.

G: Ladies and gentlemen, the temple mainly consists of the temple gate, the Heavenly King Hall, the Great Buddha Hall, the Daxiong Hall, the Jieyin Hall, Qingliang Terrace and Pilu Pavilion, which are all distributing along the north-south central axis. Let's visit it one by one.

(Standing in front of the first hall of the temple)

G: What we see now is the first hall—The Heavenly King Hall which was originally built in the Yuan Dynasty and decorated in the Qing Dynasty. There are four Heavenly Kings holding respectively a pipa, a sword, a snake and an umbrella in their hands, which symbolizing *Feng, Tiao, Yu, Shun*, a good weather for crops and peaceful country for the people. The following hall is Hall of the Great Buddha. In its center sits a statue of Sakyamuni Buddha flanked by figures of Manjusri and Samantabhadra. The third hall is Daxiong Hall which has three Buddhas. Sakyamuni is sitting in the center with Medicine Buddha who is from the Eastern Pure Land on the left and Amitabha Buddha, the teacher of the Western Pure Land on the right. The artistic treasures of the Yuan Dynasty are vivid in modeling and graceful in painting. The next hall is Jieyin Hall. Amitabha Buddha who is in charge of the Western Paradise is worshipped in this hall. It is the smallest hall in the temple. Behind the bamboo forest is the Qingliang Terrace where stands prominent on the terrace. The terrace was the first place at which Buddhist sutras were translated in China and for this reason, it is one of the most famous locations in the temple. Outside the temple, there is a tiered brick pagoda named Qiyun Pagoda, which is actually the oldest of China's ancient pagodas.

T: This temple is really amazing. After hearing your introduction, I am deeply impressed by the grandeur of temple and profound significance of Buddhism. So splendid! Thanks for your good introduction.

G: You are welcome. I am very glad you like it.

Knowledge improvement

From the very beginning, temple does not refer to Buddhist temple. Official residences were called temples in ancient times. Since Han Dynasty, Buddhism has been popular in China. In order to show respect for Buddhism, Chinese people called the Buddhist architecture as temple. Temples are placed main shrines. There are usually three main shrines in a temple, and there may be smaller ones as well in other parts of the temple.

Worship in Chinese temples usually consists of making offerings to the various gods, spirits and ancestors.

The White Horse Temple enjoys the reputation of the No.1 Ancient Temple of China. It lies on the south of Mangshan Mountain, and faces the Luohe River in the south. The White Horse Temple in today is a rectangle courtyard facing south. Covering a total area of 40000 square meters. A stone archway has been built 150 meters recently in front of the original gate. Between the archway and gate lies a pool with fountains, spanned by three stone bridges. The temple mainly consists of the temple gate, the Heavenly King Hall, the Great Buddha Hall, the Daxiong Hall, the Jieyin Hall, Qingliang Terrace and Pilu Pavilion, which are all distributing along the north-south central axis.

Activity 1: Group discussion.

All the students in the classroom are divided into several groups to discuss what important information about the White Horse Temple are mentioned in the dialogue, after discussion, each group choose a representative to make a presentation, and then the teacher should gives the comments on the students' answer.

Activity 2: Make up a dialogue.

Please practice the dialogue for 5 minutes with your deskmates. After that, teacher names some students to choose a role to make up a dialogue and then give comments on their performance if necessary.

Activity 3: Simulated guiding.

All the students in the classroom are divided into several groups, and every group member may try to act as a local guide in class to simulate a situation of introducing a familiar temple. Some phrases and expressions you have learnt may be used in your commentary.

Part C   Reading

Words List

integral	/ˈintigrəl/	adj.	完整的；不可缺的
spiritual	/ˈspiritʃuəl/	adj.	精神的；心灵的
enhance	/inˈhɑːns/	v.	提高；增强
coexist	/ˌkəuigˈzist/	v.	共存
ideological	/ˌaidiəˈlɔdʒikəl/	adj.	意识形态的；思想体系的
sutra	/ˈsuːtrə/	n.	佛经

Unit 3 Chinese Religions

astronomy	/əˈstrɒnəmi/	n.	天文学
inhabit	/ɪnˈhæbɪt/	n.	居住在；栖居于
noble	/ˈnəʊbl/	n.	贵族
disciple	/dɪˈsaɪpl/	n.	信徒；门徒
gospel	/ˈɡɒspl/	n.	福音
crucify	/ˈkruːsɪfaɪ/	v.	把某人钉在十字架上处死
resurrect	/ˌrezəˈrekt/	v.	复活；起死回生
miracle	/ˈmɪrəkəl/	n.	奇迹
Bible	/ˈbaɪbl/	n.	圣经
militarist	/ˈmɪlɪtərɪst/	n.	军事家
submission	/səbˈmɪʃn/	n.	屈服；归顺
Muslim	/ˈmʊzlɪm/	n.	穆斯林；伊斯兰教徒
doctrine	/ˈdɒktrɪn/	n.	教义；信条
convince	/kənˈvɪns/	v.	说服；劝说
advocate	/ˈædvəkeɪt/	v.	拥护；支持
manifest	/ˈmænɪfest/	v.	表明；清楚显示
maxim	/ˈmæksɪm/	n.	格言；座右铭
comprise	/kəmˈpraɪz/	v.	包含；构成
righteousness	/ˈraɪtʃəsnɪs/	n.	公正；正直
propriety	/prəˈpraɪəti/	n.	礼节；规矩
trustworthiness	/ˈtrʌstˌwɜːðinɪs/	n.	值得信赖；可靠
uphold	/ʌpˈhəʊld/	v.	支持；维护
paternalistic	/pəˌtɜːnəlˈɪstɪk/	adj.	专制的；家长作风的
sovereign	/ˈsɒvrɪn/	n.	君主；元首
benevolent	/bəˈnevələnt/	adj.	慈善的；行善的
obedient	/əˈbiːdiənt/	adj.	顺从的；恭顺的
priesthood	/ˈpriːsthʊd/	n.	牧师职位
creed	/kriːd/	n.	信念；宗教信仰

Useful Expressions

reach peak	达到顶峰
be prevalent in	盛行
put emphasis on	把重点放在
under the permission of	在……许可之下
derive from	起源于
pay taxes	纳税
be regarded as	被视为
hand down	把……往下传
suffer from	遭受
show appearance	显现

arouse great interest	引起极大的兴趣
filial piety	孝道

Proper Nouns

Siddhatha Gautam	悉达多 乔达摩
Mahayana Buddhism	大乘佛教
Hinayana Buddhism	小乘佛教
Tibetan Buddhism	藏传佛教
Lamaism	喇嘛教
Pure Land Sect	净土宗
Chan (Zen) Sect	禅宗
Pali Buddhism	巴利语系佛教
The Water-Splashing Festival	泼水节
Nyingma (Red Sect)	宁玛派
Gelug (Yellow Sect)	格鲁派
Kagyu (White Sect)	噶举派
Bon (Black Sect)	噶当派
Sakya (Striped Sect).	萨迦派
Tsongkapa	宗喀巴
Jesus	耶稣
Holy Spirit	圣灵
Roman Catholic Church	罗马天主教
the Orthodox Church	东正教
Protestantism	新教
Matteo Ricci	利玛窦
British Baptist Robert Morrison	英国传教士马礼逊
The Old Testament	旧约
the New Testament	新约
Easter Day	复活节
Christmas	圣诞节
Allah	安拉
Mohammed	穆罕默德
the Silk Road	丝绸之路
Ramadan	斋月
Lesser Bairam	开斋节
Corban Festival	古尔邦节
Mohammed's Birthday	圣纪节
the Spring and Autumn Period	春秋时期

Unit 3 Chinese Religions

the Four Books　　　　　四书
the Five Classics　　　　五经

Chinese Religions

Chinese religious culture with its own characteristics is an integral part of the whole Chinese traditional culture while has been reflecting people's spiritual life. The creative processes of religious culture enhance national confidence and pride, which is beneficial for the further creation of brilliant Chinese civilization. As the three major religions, Buddhism, Christianity and Islam are coexisted in harmony in China. Confucianism, the great philosophy and ideological system, has been influencing the thinking pattern and behavior of Chinese people from generation to generation.

Buddhism

Buddhism is one of the great living religions with more than 280 million Buddhists in the world. It was founded by Siddhatha Gautam(also called Sakyamuni) in India between the 6th and 5th century B.C.. Siddhatha Gautam was originally a prince of ancient India, he has been married a princess and had a baby. One day the prince went out of the four gates in a carriage meeting an old man, a patient, a dead man and a monk, and he decided to find ways to relieve people of sufferings. After his five-year visit and six-year cultivation, he became a Buddha known as Sakyamuni.

Nowadays, Buddhism can be divided into three types in China, including Mahayana Buddhism, Hinayana Buddhism and Tibetan Buddhism.

Mahayana Buddhism was introduced into China in the reign of Emperor Mingdi of Eastern Han Dynasty (the 1st century), the central regions for preaching and spreading were Chang'an and Luoyang where the earliest Buddhist temple (White Horse Temple) was built. Mahayana Buddhism reached its peak of popularity during the Tang Dynasty (618A.D.—907A.D.), a lot of Buddhist architecture like temples, pagodas and grottoes were constructed at that time. Meanwhile, many Buddhists from China and India began to communicate with each other, a great deal of Buddhist sutra was brought back and translated. So Buddhism has a great influence on China's philosophy, literature, painting, sculpture, music, astronomy and etc. Mahayana Buddhism stresses the existence of countless Buddhas. There are eight major sects of Mahayana Buddhism, among which the Pure Land Sect and the Chan (Zen) Sect are the most popular ones in China. Mt. Wutai in Shanxi province, Mt. Emei in Sichuan province, Mt. putuo in Zhejiang province and Mt. Jiuhua in Anhui province are the Four Great Buddhist Mountains in China.

Hinayana Buddhism, introduced from Burmin in the 7th century, is prevalent in the regions inhabited by the Dai, Bulang and Achang people in Yunnan province. It is also called Pali Buddhism because Pali is the language that was spoken in the temples in ancient

India. Hinayana Buddhiam puts emphasis on the belief that Sakyamuni is the only Buddha in the world. The local culture and some customs are also affected greatly by the religious belief. For example, young boys of Dai people have to experience the life of being a monk, they study in the temples in their school age. The Water-Splashing Festival was originally a Buddhist festival for the Dai people, but now it is the New Year's Day for them.

Tibetan Buddhiam, also known as Lamaism, is a form of Buddhism combined with Tibetan religion. Its development can be divided into two periods: the former period (the 7th century—838 A.D.) and the later period. Tibetan Buddhiam was formed officially in 978 A.D. when Buddhism was introduced into Tibet again. From then on, the different sects developed quickly, forming five leading sects: Nyingma(Red Sect), Gelug (Yellow Sect), Kagyu (White Sect), Bon (Black Sect) and Sakya (Striped Sect). Among which the Gelug was the most powerful one with larger followers under the support of the Mogol nobles and the Qing Dynasty government. It was founded by Tsongkapa in 1392 and took charge of Tibet from the middle of the 17th century.

Christianity

Christianity, found by Jesus in the first century, is a global religion with the most believers and disciples in the world. According to the records, Jesus is the son of God, and he was born by Mary who had a baby by the Holy Spirit. Jesus preached the gospel and cured many people who suffered from all kinds of diseases, he was finally crucified for giving offence to people in authority. It was said that Jesus resurrected on the 3rd day after his death. He showed appearance to his disciples and presented many other miracles in their presence, then he went to the heaven. Christianity consists of three principal divisions: Roman Catholic Church, the Orthodox Church and Protestantism.

Christianity has been entered China in four periods in Chinese history. The first period was in the Tang Dynasty (635 A.D.), but it disappeared when Emperor Wuzong forbad Buddhism. Yuan Dynasty wsa the second period for Christianity to be introduced, It was called "the Cross". And with the demise of Yuan Dynasty, Christianity died itself. Christianity was spread into China again in the Ming Dynasty (1582 A.D.). Under the permission of the Ming emperors, the Jesuit priest Matteo Ricci was allowed to build churches in Beijing, at the same time, he brought the knowledge about physics, math and astronomy to the Imperial Court. In 1807, the fourth period, Protestantism was brought to China by the British Baptist Robert Morrison. Both Roman Catholic and Protestantism developed a lot after the Opium War in 1840.

The Bible is the scripture of Christianity, including the Old Testament and the New Testament. Its symbol is a cross, the important festivals are Easter Day (the first Sunday after a full moon on or between 21st March and 25th April) and Christmas (on 25th December).

Unit 3　Chinese Religions

Islam

Islam was established in the 7th century by Mohammed who was a great Arabia religionist, thinker, politician and militarist. The name of Islam is derived from the Arabic word "Salam", which means "peace" and "submission". It implies that followers should submit oneself to the only Allah.

Islam was first introduced into China in the Tang Dynasty (651 A.D.). During the Tang and Song Dynasties, the communication between China and Arabic countries reach the peak, some famous mosques were built at that time, and some Islamic believers from Arab came over to northern China by the Silk Road to develop business trade.

The believers of Islam are called Muslim. The Koran is the scripture of Islam. Muslims abide by the doctrines seriously. For instance, they pray five times daily: at dawn, at noon, in the afternoon, in the evening and at nightfall and pay taxes to help the poor. Muslims are not allowed to eat between dawn and sunset during Ramadan, namely September of the Islamic calendar and must obey the ethics.

Chinese Muslims live mostly in the areas of the Xinjiang Uyhur Autonomous Region and Ningxia Hui Autonomous Region. Their leading Islamic festivals are Lesser Bairam, Corban Festival and Mohammed's Birthday.

Confucianism

Developed from the teachings of the great Chinese philosopher Confucius and his disciples, Confucianism is a major Chinese system of thought in China. Confucius is regarded as a great sage of China, who was born at Qufu in the State of Lu (what is now Shandong province) in about 551 B.C. and died in 479 B.C..He lived at the end of the Spring and Autumn Period, and he wandered about from state to state in order to convince the rulers of the right method to govern.

The main works of Confucianism are the Four Books and the Five Classics which were handed down by Confucius and his disciples. The Four Books, compilations of the sayings of Confucius and Mencius and of commentaries by followers on their teachings, consist of the following works: Lunyu (The Analects of Confucius), Daxue (The Great Learning), Zhongyong (The Doctrine of the Mean) and Mengzi (The Book of Mencius). The Four Classics, which originated before the time of Confucius, include Yijing (Classic of Changes), Shujing (Classic of History), Shijing (Classic of Peotry), Liji (Classic of Rites) and Chunqiu (Spring and Autumn Annals).

The core of Confucian ethics is Ren(benevolence), which is a supreme virtue representing human qualities at their best. Confucianism advocated that people should love their parents, respect their elders and be kind to their brothers. In personal relations Ren is manifested in Zhong (loyalty) or faithfulness to oneself and others. The famous maxim of Confucius can express Confucianism best which goes, "do not do to others what you do not want done to yourself." Other important Confucian virtues comprise righteousness (Yi), propriety (Li), wisdom (Zhi), trustworthiness (Xin) and filial piety (Xiao). In education confucius upholds the celebrated theory that "in education, there is no class distinction". In politics Confucius advocated a paternalistic government in which the sovereign is benevolent and honorable and the subjects are obedient and respectful. The ruler should cultivate himself and become morally perfect so as to set a good example to his people.

Confucianism has affected the Chinese attitude toward life, set the patterns of living and standards of social value, and provided the background for Chinese political theories. Even if Confucianism has never existed as an established religion with churches and priesthood, it has served as the official creed for over 2000 years. Confucianism has also been spread to Japan, Korea and Vietnam and it has aroused great interest among more and more foreign scholars.

Activity 1: Choose the correct answer to complete the following sentences.

1. Buddhism can be divided into _____ types in China.
    A. 3   B. 4   C. 5
2. Mahayana Buddhism was introduced into China in _____.
    A. Western Han Dynasty   B. Eestern Han Dynasty   C. Ming Dynasty
3. The _____ is the scripture of Christianity.
    A. Sutra   B. Koran   C. Bible
4. The Muslims advocate that followers should submit oneself to the only _____.
    A. Allah   B. Sakyamuni   C. Jesus
5. _____ is the native-born religion.
    A. Buddhism   B. Confucianism   C. Islam

Activity 2: Fill in the table according to what you have learnt.

Religion	Time for Origin	Founder	Scripture	Festivals	Religious sites
Buddhism					
Christianity					
Islam					

Activity 3: Answer the following open questions in brief.

1. Do you know any other religions developed in China? What are they?
2. What features do Chinese Buddhist temples have?
3. What stories have you ever heard from the Bible?
4. How much do you know about Mohammed and Allah?
5. What can you learn from Confucianism?

Unit 3 Chinese Religions

Part D Writing

Compose a Welcome Speech

欢迎词是导游树立良好第一印象的关键所在，也是导游拉近与游客的距离、消除陌生感的重要武器，便于在游览途中驾驭团队。因此，致欢迎词是给客人留下"第一印象"的极佳机会。

欢迎词一般包括以下部分。

(1) 称谓。称谓通常可采用"女士们，先生们"、"各位嘉宾"、"各位贵宾"等。

(2) 表示欢迎。对游客的到来表示热烈的欢迎，通常可采用"welcome to (某城市)"、"on behalf of (某旅行社)，I would like to extend a warm welcome to you"。

(3) 自我介绍。向游客介绍自己和司机，并且表示愿意竭尽全力为他们提供优质的服务。

(4) 介绍时差。向游客介绍时差，并建议他们把时间调整为北京时间。

(5) 城市概况。从地理、历史、经济、餐饮等各方面对游客所到的城市进行详细介绍。

(6) 行程安排。向游客介绍具体的行程，并核实此行程与游客的行程是否一致，如果不一致应向旅行社负责人报告。

(7) 天气预报。对未来几日的天气情况进行介绍，并提醒游客及时增减衣服、携带雨具等。

(8) 下榻酒店。介绍游客所下榻酒店的地理位置及内部设施等。

(9) 两个号码。自己的手机号码(cellphone number)和旅游车的车牌号码(plate number)。

(10) 提醒。提醒游客在旅游期间要注意安全，证件和贵重物品应随身携带。小心扒手，不要直接饮用自来水等。

(11) 结语。结词通常都是些祝愿性的语言。"I hope you will enjoy your stay in Beijing"或"I hope you will have a very pleasant stay here"。

另外，欢迎词注意汲取一些谚语、名言，充满文采的欢迎词会收到很好效果，下面一些谚语可参考使用："有朋自远方来，不亦乐乎"；"百年修得同船渡"；"有缘千里来相会"；"世界像部书，如果您没出外旅行，您可只读了书中之一页，现在您在我们这里旅行，让我们共同读好中国的这一页"。

Sample

Situation：A tour group from Canada arrives at Beijing International Airport. Miss Li Xiaohua, a local guide from China Beijing International Travel Service, meets them at the airport. After she helps tourists claim the luggage and get on the coach, she delivers a welcome speech to the tourists on behalf of China Beijing International Travel Service.

Welcome Speech

Good evening, ladies and gentlemen!

Welcome to Beijing! First of all, please allow me to introduce my team. My name is Li Xiaohua, you can also call me Miss Li. I am from China Beijing International Travel Service, and I will be your local guide in Beijing. Mr. Zhang is our bus driver, he has more than 10 years of driving under his belt, so you are in very safe hands. During your stay in Beijing, we will do everything possible to make your trip more enjoyable. If you have any difficulties, please do not hesitate to let us know, we will try our best to help you. I hope you will have a pleasant experience in Beijing.

Even though China spans 5 time zones, we only have one time——Beijing standard time all through china. The time difference is 16 hours between Beijing and San Francisco, so please reset your watches. Now Beijing standard time is 9:30 p.m.

It is about one hour's ride from the airport to the hotel. Now I would like to tell you something about our itinerary for the coming two days. Tomorrow we will visit the Palace Museum in the morning and the Temple of Heaven in the afternoon and we will enjoy the famous Beijing opera in the evening. The day after tomorrow we will visit the Great Wall in the morning and the Ming Tombs in the afternoon. Then you will take an evening flight to Shanghai.

You are going to stay at Holiday Inn Lidu Hotel for two nights, it is a luxurious, five-star hotel. Bags of tea and coffee in your rooms are complimentary, and you can also purchase drinks from the mini bar. You can make exchange money at the hotel. please boil the tap water before you drink, because it may not be drinkable.

We shall meet at the lobby at 7:30 a.m. for our first visit. Please do remember the plate number of our bus—56798, and my cell phone number is 13933666999. Hope you will have a good trip in Beijing!

Simulated Writing

Directions: Please use the words, phrases or expressions you have learnt to write a welcome speech according to the Chinese tips, the main contents should include extending warm welcome, team-introduction, general situation of the city, itinerary design, hotel facilities introduction, two numbers and ending sentences.

女士们，先生们：

早上好！我叫李丽，首先我代表中国国际旅行社北京分社对您的到来表示最热烈的欢迎！非常荣幸地担任你们这次来华的导游。这位是司机赵先生，他是一位有丰富驾驶经验的司机。各位在北京游览期间，我们将竭诚为诸位服务，如果您在旅游过程中遇到困难，请您一定要通知我们，我们会竭尽所能给予帮助。

北京和旧金山的时差是16个小时，请您重置手表，现在是北京标准时间下午9:30。我们下榻的酒店是丽都假日酒店，该酒店位于市中心，是装饰考究、服务一流的五星

Unit 3　Chinese Religions

级酒店。从机场到我们丽都假日酒店大约是一个小时的车程，下面我将向大家简单地介绍一下日程安排……最后请大家记住我们的车号34308以及我的电话13911113333。预祝大家能在北京度过一个舒适、愉快而难忘的旅程。谢谢大家！

Part E　Practical Training

Training item 1: Oral Presentation

Directions: You are required to work with your group members to finish the task in this part. Every group should choose a kind of religion you are familiar to give an introduction. After preparation and practice, a group member will be asked to make an oral presentation, other students may have additional remarks or explanation if necessary. And then the teacher gives comments on the students' performance.

Training item 2: Role-play

Directions: All the students in the class are divided into several groups, every member in the group choose one role to perform. Students should use the language they have learnt as far as possible.

Situation 1: Ms. Brown, a tourist from USA, comes to Henan province. A local guide Lily is showing her around White Horse Temple—a very famous Buddhist temple in China. Lily is introducing the knowledge of Chinese Temples like the layout, structure, the Buddhist figures of worship in the hall, etc.

Situation 2: Ms. Brown is very interested in Buddhism, and a local guide Lily is giving her brief introduction of Buddhism. In addition, Lily offers her more knowledge about other religions like native-born Confucianism.

Situation 3: Lily, a local guide from China Henan International Travel Service, is providing tourists from England with meeting service at the airport. Now, she is delivering a warm welcome speech.

Training item 3: Outside-class Work

Directions: Please find some information about other famous temples or pagodas in China from books, Internet or some other channels. Try to compare and explain some characteristics of them and then make a brief introduction.

Knowledge links

Three Kinds of Buddhist Architectural Forms

Grottoes

There are three greatest grottoes in China, including Mogao Grottoes at Dunhuang in Gansu province, Yungang Grottoes at Datong in Shanxi provicne, and Longmen Grottoes at Luoyang in Henan province.

Temples

Three famous temples in China are White Horse Temple in Luoyang city; Lingyin Temple in Hangzhou city; Shaolin Temple in Dengfeng County.

Pagodas

Several Chinese ancient pagodas still standing are as follows: Three Pagodas of Chongshan Temple in Yunnan province, Yingxian Wooden Pagoda in Shanxi province, Big Wild Goose Pagoda in Shaanxi province, Kaifeng Iron Pagoda in Henan province, Leifeng Pagoda in Zhejiang province and Huqiu Pagoda in Jiangsu province.

Four Sacred Buddhist Mountains

Mount Wutai

Mount Wutai is situated in northeast Wutai County of Shanxi province. It is believed to be the sacred place where Manjusri lived and preached, and it tops the other three Buddhist Mountains in China. What's more, Mount Wutai is the only shrine in China where Mahayana Buddhism and Tibetan Buddhism coexist.

Mount Emei

Situated 165 kilometers from Chengdu, Sichuan province, Mount Emei is the sacred place where Samantabhadra preached. Buddhism arrived at Mount Emei about 2000 years ago and left behind over 30 temples. Sunrise, Buddhist halo and sea of clouds are the three wonders of Mount Emei.

Mount Putuo

Mount Putuo is the sacred place where Avalokitesvara (Guanyin or Goddess of Mercy) lived. As the legend goes, Avalokitesvara once showed her bodily presence here and left a lot of celebrated historical sites. Many beautiful names were given to Mount Putuo such as "Buddhist Paradise on the Sea", "Land of Peach Blossoms", etc. The most famous temple at Mount Putuo is "Unwilling to Leave Nunnery".

Mount Jiuhua

Located in Anhui province, Mount Jiuhua is believed to be the sacred place for Ksitigarbha to live and preach. There were more than 300 temples with over 4000 monks at the mountain during the heyday in history. Mount Jiuhua is esteemed as the Fairy City of Buddhist Kingdom.

Famous churches in China

The well-known churches in China are St. Sophia Church in Harbin, Heilongjiang province, Shanghai International Church, Shanghai Notre Dame Cathedral, Guangzhou Sacred Heart Cathedral etc.

Four famous Islamic Mosques

The four famous Islamic mosques in China are Huaisheng Mosque (怀圣寺) in Guangdong province, Qingjing Mosque (清净寺) in Fujian province, Fenghuang Mosque (凤凰寺) in Zhejiang province and Xianhe Mosque (仙鹤寺) in Jiangsu province.

Chinese Ancient Architecture

Unit 4

Topic Guidance

Chinese architecture can be categorized into imperial palaces, temples, gardens, mausoleums and residential houses, city walls.

Chinese architecture is a continuation of a unique system for thousands of years, which made it have its own unique traditions.

The Humble Administrator's Garden in Suzhou is a typical of architecture style south of Yangze River.

A good Tour Commentary should include tile, route, extending warm welcome, brief introduction, spot introduction, and conclusion.

Warming-up

Read the following questions and discuss with your partner.

1. How much do you know about the Chinese ancient architecture?
2. Could you name some famous ancient architecture in China?
3. Is there any ancient architecture in your hometown? Would you introduce some?

Look at the following pictures and try to describe it in your own words.

Part A   Listening

Words List

Structure	/ˈstrʌktʃə(r)/	n.	建筑物；结构
construction	/kənˈstrʌkʃn/	n.	建造物；构筑物；
decisive	/diˈsaisiv/	adj.	决定性的；关键的
influence	/ˈinfluəns/	n.	影响；作用
civilization	/ˌsivəlaiˈzeiʃn/	n.	文明
architecture	/ˈɑːkitektʃə(r)/	n.	建筑设计；建筑风格
continuation	/kənˌtinjuˈeiʃn/	n.	继续；连续；
terrace	/ˈterəs/	n.	露天平台；阳台
hierarchy	/ˈhaiərɑːki/	n.	等级制度
timber	/ˈtimbə(r)/	n.	木材，木料
framework	/ˈfreimwəːk/	n.	构架，框架，结构
improvement	/imˈpruːvmənt/	n.	改善；改进
mural	/ˈmjuərəl/	n.	壁画
monograph	/ˈmɔnəgrɑːf/	n.	专论；专题文章；专著
manual	/ˈmænjuəl/	adj.	用手的；手工的；体力的
peak	/piːk/	n.	顶峰；高峰
mausoleum	/ˌmɔːsəˈliːəm/	n.	陵墓
element	/ˈelimənt/	n.	元素；要素

Useful Expressions

refer to	提及，所指
date from	自……至今
build up	建立
tend to	有……的倾向
rammed-earth	夯土
exquisite sculpture	精美的雕刻
glazed tile	琉璃瓦

Proper Nouns

primitive society	原始社会
YINGZAOFASHI	营造法式

Unit 4 Chinese Ancient Architecture

Activity 1: Spot dictation.

Chinese ancient architecture (1)_____ the buildings, structures, construction methods and related systems led by China's ancient culture without any decisive influence of modern (2)_____. Chinese ancient architecture is an important part of China's splendid (3)_____. It is a continuation of a unique system for thousands of years, which made it have its own unique traditions.

Chinese ancient architecture has been (4)_____ during the period from (5)_____ society to the Han Dynasty of ancient China. During the Xia Dynasty (6)_____ the 21st century B.C. buildings constructed with (7)_____ appeared like palaces built on high and large rammed terraces. And more important, the constructions began to show the hierarchy (8)_____ between men.

(9)_____ has become the main way of building structure since the continuous improvement of Shang and Zhou Dynasties. From the Spring and Autumn period(770—476 B.C.) to the period of the Qin (221—206 B.C.) and Han (206 B.C. —220 A.D.) Dynasties, as (10)_____ were introduced, a complete construction system was gradually built up to create the simple and open style of the early stage.

From the period of Wei (220—265) and Jin (265—420) to the period of the Southern and Northern Dynasties, the constructions developed gradually. (11)_____ such as (12)_____ and exquisite sculptures and murals were built rapidly and widely. (13) _____ Tang Dynasty, an elegant and poised style of construction has been formed. Since the Song Dynasty (960—1279), the function of architecture was more stressed to (14)_____ and its shape and appearance tended to be smooth, splendid and beautiful. The great book named "YINGZAOFASHI", a building monograph of the architectural design of manuals and technical specifications was produced. The period between Ming (1368—1644) and Qing (1644—1911) Dynasties is the last peak of (15)_____. The (16) _____ of bricks and glazed tile are much more than the ones in any previous dynasties. Several high profile buildings were constructed and improved including (17)_____ during this period.

Since ancient times, Chinese architecture has heavily (18)_____ constructions in Japan, North Korea, Vietnam, and Mongolia. Today, Chinese architecture has (19)_____ all kinds of elements from western countries and (20)_____ while preserving traditional style.

Activity 2: Decide whether the following statements are True or False while listening to the paragraph again.

(   ) 1. The architecture in China influenced by modern Western civilization is called ancient architecture.

(　　) 2. Chinese traditional culture has a great impact on the ancient architecture.

    (　　) 3. During the period of the Southern and Northern Dynasties, Buddhist constructions were very popular.

    (　　) 4. The book named "YINGZAOFASHI" is a book telling people how to protect Buddhism.

    (　　) 5. Chinese architecture has heavily influenced constructions of some Asian countries.

Activity 3: Choose the correct answer while you are listening.

1. Which countries constructions were influenced by China?
    A. Western countries   B. Asian countries   C. European countries

2. When was the Chinese ancient architecture formed?
    A. Ming Dynasty   B. Qing Dynasty   C. Shang Dynasty

3. When did China's constructions begin to show the people's hierarchy?
    A. during the Xia Dynasty
    B. during the period of Wei
    C. during Tang Dynasty

4. What is the main architectural material in Shang Dynasty?
    A. rock   B. timber   C. rammed earth

5. When was the last peak of Chinese ancient architecture?
    A. Qing Dynasty
    B. Ming Dynasty
    C. the period between Ming and Qing Dynasties

Part B　Speaking

WordS List

profundity	/prəˈfʌnditi/	n.	博大精深
constitute	/ˈkɔnstitjuːt/	n.	组成；构成
renowned	/riˈnaʊnd/	adj.	有名的；闻名的
designate	/ˈdezigneit/	v.	命名；指定
pavilion	/pəˈviliən/	n.	亭；阁
chamber	/ˈtʃeimbə(r)/	n.	房间；室
maze	/meiz/	n.	迷宫
idyllic	/iˈdiliki/	adj.	平和美丽的；完美无瑕的
storey	/ˈstɔːri/	n.	层

Unit 4 Chinese Ancient Architecture

Useful Expressions

play a very important role	起着重要的作用
lay out	展示；摆出
get lost	迷路
be divided into	被分成
float on	悬浮在……上
be eager to do sth.	渴望做某事
be dotted with	被……点缀着

Proper Nouns

China Jiangsu International Travel Service	中国江苏国际旅行社
the Humble Administrator's Garden	拙政园
World Cultural Heritage	世界文化遗产
the Summer Palace	颐和园
the Chengde Mountain Resort	承德避暑山庄
the Lingering Garden	留园
On Idle Living	《闲居赋》
Gui Tian Yuan Ju	归田园居
Fu Yuan Garden	复园
BuYuan Garden	补园
Cymbidium Goeringii Hall	兰雪堂
Celestial Spring Pavilion	天泉阁

Situational dialogue 1

Miss Wang Lina, a local guide from China Jiangsu International Travel Service, is taking American guests to visit the Chinese classic garden, the Humble Administrator's Garden in Suzhou, a typical of architecture style south of Yangze River.

  T: tourists   G: local guide

  G: Ladies and gentlemen, now what we are going to visit is a very famous Chinese classic garden, the Humble Administrator's Garden. You know, the garden architecture plays a very important role in ancient Chinese architecture.

  T: Miss Li, I have heard that this garden is a private garden. Is it right?

  G: Yes，absolutely right. The imperial garden in the north China and the private garden in south China constituted are the two major schools of Chinese garden architecture. The beautiful waterside city of Suzhou in southern China is most famous for its elegant classical private gardens. Among these, the Humble Administrator's Garden is the largest and most renowned. It is listed as a World Cultural Heritage and has also been designated as one of the cultural relics with state-level. Along with the Summer Palace in Beijing, the Mountain

Resort of Chengde in Hebei province and the Lingering Garden in Suzhou, it is considered as one of China's four most famous gardens.

T: Oh, really! How beautiful! When was it built?

G: The Humble Administrator's Garden was originally built in 1509 during the Ming Dynasty.

T: Then why is it called the "Zhuozhengyuan Garden"?

G: All right, good question. Let me tell you! It was initially laid out by a former government official named Wang Xianchen after his retirement from political life. He named the garden after an essay by Pan Yue of West Jin Dynasty—On Idle Living: "Building house and planting trees, watering garden and growing vegetables are the affairs (Zheng) of humble (Zhuo) people." So the garden got the name of "Zhuo Zheng Yuan".

T: Oh, I see. That sounds interesting.

G: Well, before you tour the garden I think you'd better remember the layout of the garden; otherwise you may get lost or miss some important scenic spots. The garden's scenery is focused on a central large pool with numerous pavilions, terraces, bridges, chambers and towers among a maze of connected pools and islands.

(Standing beside the lacquer painting)

G: Ladies and gentlemen, please look at this painting. From this, we can see that the garden could be divided into three parts. The east part Gui Tian Yuan Ju (return to nature) mainly consists of idyllic scenery. The middle part Fu Yuan is the essence of the whole garden, and its ponds and rockery are the best. The western part is called BuYuan, in which most of the buildings were built in the Qing Dynasty. All of the buildings are right next to the ponds, making the garden look like floating on the water. After you have a clear idea about the layout of the garden. I'll show you around this famous garden. Are you ready?

T: We are eager to see it at once!

G: Here we are in the eastern part. It is the first part of the garden. Here we can appreciate the main features of Suzhou classic garden. The eastern section is dotted with lush grasses, dense bamboo, overgrown plants and winding streams. It's centered on Cymbidium Goeingii Hall (Lanxue Tang), from where you can get a complete view of the garden. We are going to visit the Celestial Spring Pavilion (Tianquan Ting), named from an ancient well of sweet-lasting water. The pavilion has eight sides which are double-eaves. By the way, does anyone know how many storeys the pavilion has?

T: It has two storeys.

G: No, it is actually a one-storey structure if you examine it from inside.

T: Oh, really, so interesting. After hearing your introduction, I am deeply impressed by the beautiful scenery of the garden. So splendid! Thanks for your good introduction.

G: You are welcome. I am very glad you like it.

Unit 4　Chinese Ancient Architecture

Knowledge improvement

　　The Humble Administrator's Garden is typical of fantastic artificial landscape and well designed water space. Besides, it is full of tender family aura as well. The whole garden is the embodiment of what the ancient people had been pursuing all the time as the "Earthly Heaven" because it represents the traditional Chinese philosophical concepts of showing high ideals by simple living. The garden can be divided into three sections.

　　The central part is the quintessence of the garden, with one-third of its area covered by water. It centers on the Hall of Distant Fragrance (Yuanxiang Tang pavilion), named after a lotus pool nearby. When the summer comes, the pool is filled with lotuses and the heady fragrance wafts into the building. Two artificial islands are linked to each other through a bridge in the lotus pond north of the pavilion.

　　The main structure in the western section is a hall which is separated into two parts by a large screen. The south part is the 18 Camellias Hall (Shiba Mantuoluohua Guan Hall), and the north part is the Thirty-Six Mandarin Ducks' Hall (Sanshiliu Yuanyang Guan Hall).

Activity 1: Group discussion.

　　All the students in the classroom are divided into several groups to discuss what important information about the Humble Administrator's Garden are mentioned in the dialogue, after discussion, each group choose a representative to make a presentation, and then the teacher should give the comment on students' answer.

Activity 2: Make up a dialogue.

　　Please practice the dialogue for 5 minutes with your deskmates. After that, the teacher names some students to choose a role to make up a dialogue and then gives comments on their performance if necessary.

Activity 3: Simulated guiding.

　　All the students in the classroom are divided into several groups, and every group member may try to act as a local guide in class to simulate a situation of introducing a familiar garden. Some phrases and expressions you have learnt may be used in your commentary.

Part C　Reading

Words List

incorporate	/inˈkɔːpəreit/	v.	包含；吸收
lintel	/ˈlintl/	n.	过梁；门楣
joist	/dʒɔist/	n.	搁栅；托梁

55

imperial	/ɪmˈpɪəriəl/	adj.	皇帝的；帝国的
residential	/ˌrezɪˈdenʃəl/	adj.	住宅的；提供住宿的
layout	/ˈleɪaʊt/	n.	布局；设置
symmetry	/ˈsɪmətri/	n.	对称
axis	/ˈæksɪs/	n.	轴；对称中心线
moat	/məʊt/	n.	护城河
furnishing	/ˈfɜːnɪʃɪŋ/	n.	装饰
scatter	/ˈskætə(r)/	v.	散播；分散
symbolization	/ˌsɪmbəlaɪˈzeɪʃn/	n.	象征；表现
Mosque	/mɒsk/	n.	清真寺
humanity	/hjuːˈmænəti/	n.	人类；人性
embrace	/ɪmˈbreɪs/	v.	接收；采纳
complex	/ˈkɒmpleks/	n.	建筑群
shrine	/ʃraɪn/	n.	神龛
royalty	/ˈrɔɪəlti/	n.	王室成员
horticulture	/ˈhɔːtɪkʌltʃə(r)/	n.	园艺学；园艺
grandiose	/ˈɡrændiəʊs/	adj.	壮观的；夸张的
tasteful	/ˈteɪstfəl/	adj.	高雅的；雅致的
verdant	/ˈvɜːdnt/	adj	嫩绿的；碧绿的
majestic	/məˈdʒestɪk/	adj.	雄伟的；崇高的
funeral	/ˈfjuːnərəl/	n.	丧葬；葬礼
design	/dɪˈzaɪn/	v.	设计；构想
elaborately	/ɪˈlæbərətli/	adv.	精心的；精巧的
turret	/ˈtʌrət/	n.	角楼；塔楼；炮塔
coffin	/ˈkɒfɪn/	n.	棺材；灵柩
prevalent	/ˈprevələnt/	adj.	流行的；盛行的
enclosure	/ɪnˈkləʊʒə(r)/	n.	围住；封住；围场
pine	/paɪn/	n.	松树
cypress	/ˈsaɪprəs/	n.	柏树
solemn	/ˈsɒləm/	adj.	严肃的；庄重的
harmonious	/hɑːˈməʊniəs/	adj.	和谐的；协调的
spirituality	/ˌspɪrɪtʃuˈæləti/	n.	精神性；灵性
flexible	/ˈfleksəbl/	adj.	灵活的
withstand	/wɪðˈstænd/	v.	承受；抵住
cannon	/ˈkænən/	n.	大炮
demolish	/dɪˈmɒlɪʃ/	v.	拆毁；拆除
orthogonal	/ɔːˈθɒɡənl/	adj.	直角的；矩形的
interval	/ˈɪntəvl/	n.	间隔；间隙

Unit 4 Chinese Ancient Architecture

Useful Expressions

attach importance to	重视
based on	基于
be integrated with	与……相结合
compared with	与……相比
make an important part	成为重要的组成部分
residential house	民居
the central axis	中轴线
flowery pillar	华表
stone lion	石狮
sun dial	日晷
copper grain measure	嘉量
incense burner	香炉
bronze turtle	铜龟
bronze crane	铜鹤
a central axis	中轴线
man-made landscape	人造景观
artistic field	艺术领域
imperial mausoleums	皇家陵园
archery tower	瓮城

Proper Nouns

Kong Miao	孔庙
Wen Miao	文庙
Yonghe Lamasery	雍和宫
the temple of Heaven	天坛
corner towers	角楼

Chinese Ancient Architecture

Chinese distinctive architecture acts an important role in China's splendid civilization. It is a unity of science, creativity and arts. It not only has a unique style, but also has special features which makes it unique in the world architecture. Chinese, Western and Muslim architecture comprise the three major architectural systems in the world. Chinese architecture is rooted in cultural tradition and features several characteristics. It highlights absolute imperial power and strict social status. During the long-term of China's development, many architectural wonders have been created by clever and industrious Chinese laboring people. Chinese architecture stresses overall beauty and incorporates elements of nature. The axial layout pattern is widely used in all kinds of architectural buildings. The Chinese style also incorporates elements of nature and emphasizes a graceful reserved and easy-going beauty.

The framework of a house in ancient architecture is usually made up by wooden posts, beams, lintels and joists. With the time went up, Chinese architecture gradually formed into a style that featured timberwork combining stone carving, rammed earth construction, bucket arch buildings and many other techniques. Chinese architecture can be categorized into imperial palaces, temples, gardens, mausoleums and residential houses, city walls.

Imperial Palaces

Imperial palace is a very important type of Chinese traditional architecture. Imperial palace is a group of buildings in which the emperor lived and worked in the ancient times, and it grew ever larger in scale in Qing Dynasty.

The layout of palace has several characteristics as follows: First of all, palace architecture is based on the principle of symmetry strictly. The main buildings are set along the central axis, and the secondary structures are positioned on either side to form yards. What's more, palace is surrounded by one or more city walls and moats. The main buildings are built on high terrace, facing the south. Furthermore, office buildings are set in the front of the palace, while the living accommodations of the imperial family and imperial garden are set at the back of the palace. Eventually, furnishings are scattered in and outside of the palace, such as flowery pillar, stone lion, sun dial, copper grain measure, vat, incense burner, bronze turtle, bronze crane, etc.

Temples

Temples are the symbolization of the long history and rich culture of China, and are regarded as valuable art treasures. Chinese temples can refer to any temples which are used for the practice of Chinese folk religions. Buddhist temples include a temple, pagoda and grotto, which are called Si (寺), Ta (塔), and Shiku (石窟) in Chinese respectively. Taoist architecture is variously called Gong (宫), Guan (观) or An (庵) in Chinese. In Confucianism, the temple is called Miao, Gong, or Tan in Chinese, for example, Kong Miao, Wen Miao, Yonghe Lamasery, the temple of Heaven, etc.. An Islamic house of worship is referred to as a Mosque. In Catholicism, the temple is called church.

Chinese temples want to express the concept of the integration of heaven and humanity, that is, human beings is a part of nature. Followed by this idea, many Chinese temples actively embrace themselves into nature. This is why so many Chinese temples are located in mountains and forests.

In most Chinese Buddhist temples, the complex buildings stand on a central axis, usually a north-south axis and east-west only acts as an exception. The main buildings are strung along this central axis. The most important and most frequently presented building

Unit 4 Chinese Ancient Architecture

inside a Buddhist temple complex are the main entrance gate, the bell and drum towers, the Hall of the Heavenly Kings, the Hall of the Buddha and a pagoda.

Cultural artifacts of every dynasty are well kept in Chinese Temple in our country. And temple culture has influenced every aspect of Chinese people's life such as astronomy, geography, architecture, painting, handwriting, sculpture, music, dancing, antiquity, temple fairs, and folk customs and so on.

Gardens

Gardens are the places to provide people with leisure and entertainment, which act an important role in China's ancient architecture. It is a combining structure of manmade landscape and natural scenery. Chinese gardens have a long history which may date back to Shang and Zhou Dynasties. In the following dynasties, building gardens became a fashion. The private garden was not appeared until the Han Dynasty. In the Qing Dynasty, garden architecture reached its peak.

Chinese traditional gardens were basically built by royalty and nobles and were used for leisure and entertainment. There are plants and trees, flowers and birds, mountains and waters, and pavilions in the gardens. A Chinese garden usually mixes man-made landscape with natural scenery, architecture, painting, literature, calligraphy, and horticulture.

There are two major schools of Chinese garden architecture, which are the imperial garden in the north China and the private garden in the south China. The imperial gardens are usually spacious, grandiose, and were built for royal families by thousands of people and perform diverse functions. Private gardens are generally small in size, but look elegant and tasteful.

Besides the former two categories of gardens, monastic gardens and garden architecture in scenic resorts also shows their splendid and beautiful sceneries. The monastic gardens which are filled with sacred atmosphere are commonly found in monasteries against quiet and verdant mountains.

Mausoleums

Mausoleums are the most majestic and largest building complexes and make an important part in ancient Chinese architectures. Old Chinese people commonly attached importance to the funeral based on the belief that the spirit dose not die with the body. Therefore, every class of the society designed the mausoleums elaborately with different style. The Chinese mausoleum buildings have got rapid development in endless course of history. Usually, the mausoleums are integrated with various art forms, such as painting, calligraphy, carving and so on.

The tomb chambers usually used wood, brick and stone as the main building materials. The forms have been changing as the times replaced. The overall arrangements of Chinese mausoleums always include walls around, doors opened to four directions, as well as turrets on four corners. Coffins with exterior wooden enclosure were prevalent before Western Zhou Dynasty. Covering large scales and a big mound with a wide base is a typical representation of Qin and Han Dynasty. During Tang Dynasty, a peak of building mausoleums in China's history, the mausoleums were built against a mountain. Mausoleums in Song Dynasty were smaller and emperors of Yuan Dynasty were buried according to Mongolian customs. Ming Dynasty is another climax of building tombs in China's history, Ming tombs are always surrounded by mountains. There is usually a paved path leading to the tomb with stone persons and stone beast on both sides. Many trees, usually pines and cypresses are planted around the mausoleums adding solemn, respectful and quiet atmosphere. Qing Dynasty is the glorious period in the history of Chinese ancient mausoleum as it added the idea of the harmonious unity of mausoleum construction with nature.

Residential Houses

Residential houses are not only an important type of Chinese traditional architecture but also a key component in ancient folk architecture system in China. Residential houses are to meet the needs of residence. However, compared with palaces and temples, their function of spirituality is not remarkable. Residential architecture has shown its variety of artistic styles in the general layout, architectural form and space composition.

Unlike building the official architectures, people construct their own houses only by self-wisdom and demands as well as inherent law in architecture according to local condition, economic standard and the characteristics of architectural materials. Therefore, the residential houses are characterized by practical function, flexible design, economical building materials and simple external forms.

Generally speaking, Chinese residential houses can be divided into three types. One is the northern residential houses; the other is the southern residential houses; another is the house in minority nationality regions of China.

In the process of thousand years, Chinese people have accumulated more experience of building residential houses. In order to have an ideal living environment, people in different places created residential houses with various forms. In view of distinct architectural forms, residential houses in some areas have shown a trend of diversification.

City Walls

Chinese ancient city walls refer to civic defensive systems used to protect towns and cities in ancient times. The wall system consisted of walls, gates, barbican, towers, and moat, which were often built to a uniform standard throughout the Empire. Like various other innovations in Chinese architecture history, the city walls also play an important part in

Unit 4 Chinese Ancient Architecture

Chinese architecture. The construction of the city wall can be traced back to Xia Dynasty and grew to a peak in the Ming Dynasty and Qing Dynasty. Sophisticated construction techniques could make the city withstand cannon fire. However with the development of efficient trade and intercourse, many city walls were almost completely demolished.

Chinese city walls are rectangular in shape, with four orthogonal walls. Some wall systems are composed of a number of rectangles. The walls could be constructed with a variety of materials. Common materials included rammed earth, compressed earth blocks, brick, stone, and any combination of these. Gates were placed symmetrically along the walls. The principal gate was traditionally located at the centre of the south wall. Gatehouses were generally built of wood and brick. A tunnel ran under the gatehouse, with several metal grates and wooden doors. An "archery tower" was often placed in front of the main gatehouse, forming a barbican. In its final form during the Ming and Qing Dynasties, the archery tower was an elaborate construction, of comparable height to the main gatehouse, which stands some distance in front of the main gatehouse. Towers that protruded from the wall were located at regular intervals along the wall. Large and elaborate towers, called corner towers, were placed where two walls joined. These were significantly higher than the wall itself, and gave defenders a bird's eye view over both the city and its surroundings. In larger cities, a moat usually surrounds the wall. This could be connected to canals or rivers both in the city and outside, thus providing both a defense and a convenient transportation route. Nearby waterways might be adopted to form part of the moat.

Activity 1: Choose the correct answer to complete the following sentences.

1. There are _____ major types of garden in China.
    A. 4   B. 3   C. 2
2. Northern residential houses, _____ residential houses and the house in minority nationality regions of China make up the three types of Chinese residential houses.
    A. Western   B. Eastern   C. Southern
3. Kong Miao is _____ temple.
    A. Buddhism   B. Confucianism   C. Islam
4. The main buildings of imperial palace are set along the _____ axis.
    A. either   B. front   C. central
5. Summer palace belongs to _____ garden.
    A. private   B. monastic   C. royal

Activity 2: Fill in the table according to what you have learnt.

Architecture form	Time for Origin	Features	Representatives
imperial palaces			
temples			

gardens			
mausoleums			
residential houses			
city walls			

Activity 3: Answer the following open questions in brief.

1. Do you know any other architecture forms built in China? What are they?
2. What features do Chinese royal gardens have?
3. Could you introduce a kind of Chinese architecture according to what you have learned?
4. How much do you know about architecture materials?
5. How many types can Chinese residential houses be divided into?

Part D Writing

Develop a Tour Commentary

导游词是导游讲解的基础。导游只有在进行多方面资料搜集的基础上进行实地考察，并争取运用导游词撰写技巧，才能不断提升自己撰写导游词的水平，通过优质的讲解提高带团能力。一篇完整的导游词通常由3部分组成，即标题、导游线路、正文。这其中，正文由以下内容组成：前言、总述、分述和结尾。

1. 前言部分通常是导游在陪同游客参观、游览前，问候大家、欢迎大家并做自我介绍的话，既简短、亲切，又要起到引出下文的作用。

2. 总述部分是对将要参观游览的景点用精练的词句进行的整体介绍，让游客初步对景点有所了解，以便让游客有一种见树先见林的感觉。

3. 分述部分是导游词的重点，是按游览的先后顺序，对所到景观逐一进行生动、具体的讲述，使游客尽情饱览一个个景点的风韵和艺术魅力。每一个大景点通常由许多小景点组成，导游词的讲解要注意把重点放在最具有代表性的景点和景物上，不需要也不可能面面俱到。

4. 结尾就是导游词的结束语，包括简短总结、回顾、感谢、美好祝愿和期待再次游览。

一篇优秀的导游词，除了要求结构严谨、层次清晰、文字流畅外，还有以下要求。

1. 知识性。一篇优秀的导游词必须有丰富的内容，融入各类知识并旁征博引、融会贯通、引人入胜。导游词不能只满足于一般性介绍，还要注重深层次的内容，如同类事物的鉴赏、有关诗词的点缀、名家的评论等，这样，会提高导游词的档次水准。

2. 准确性。导游词的内容必须准确无误，令人信服。不能随意编造，以地摊文学为蓝本，编造一些稀奇古怪、更改历史、子虚乌有的故事。

Unit 4 Chinese Ancient Architecture

3. 口语性。在创作导游词时，要注意多用口语词汇和浅显易懂的书面语词汇。避免晦涩难懂的书面语词汇和音节拗口的词汇。多用短句，以便讲起来顺口，听起来轻松。

4. 趣味性。一篇幽默风趣的导游词能给游客带来欢声笑语，创造一种其乐融融的美好氛围。要注重编织故事情节，语言生动形象，用词丰富多变。恰当地运用修辞方法，言之有情，随机应变，临场发挥。

5. 重点性。导游词必须在照顾全面的情况下突出重点。面面俱到，没有重点的导游词是不成功的。

6. 针对性。导游词不是以一代百、千篇一律的。它必须是从实际以发，因人、因时而异的，要有的放矢，即根据不同的游客以及当时的情绪和周围的环境进行导游讲解。

7. 层次性。导游词要有层次感，即在介绍景点的地理位置、历史背景时，要层层叠进，思路清楚。

8. 方向性。由于导游在介绍景点时，往往站在一个特定的位置，根据不同方位向游客介绍，所以导游词还必须具备方向感，也就是使用"在游客朋友的右边……"此类语句。

Sample

Situation： A tour group from Canada will visit Pingyao ancient city in Shanxi province. Miss Li Xiaohua, a local guide from Shanxi International Travel Service, will meet them and take them to visit the Pingyao ancient city. Before the tourists arrive, she must write some suitable guide words of Pingyao ancient city. The important tour site is the Pingyao ancient city wall.

Pingyao Ancient City Wall

Good evening, ladies and gentlemen!

Welcome to Shanxi! First of all, please allow me to introduce myself. My name is Li Xiaohua, you can also call me Miss Li or Xiao Li. I am from China Shanxi International Travel Service, and I will be your local guide in Shanxi.

Our today's destination is Pingyao Ancient city which has been formally named as "World Cultural Heritage" by UNESCO. It lies in middle of Shanxi , 90 kilometers from Taiyuan. The city has a history of 2800 years. In ancient time, it was called Gutao. It keeps all the features of the cities of Chinese Han nationality during the Ming and Qing Dynasties, displaying a complete picture of the unusual cultural, social, economic and religious development. Pingyao is known mainly for three historical treasures: the ancient brick city wall, the Zhenguo Temple, and the Shuanglin Temple.

The city wall of Pingyao was originally built using rammed earth, and was rebuilt with bricks in 1370 during the reign of Emperor Hong Wu of the Ming Dynasty. Now we have arrived at the North Gate of the city. Let's go up to the ancient wall to have a look. Please follow me. Here is the map of the city. You can find the southern gate of the city is like the head of a tortoise. The two wells outside the gate symbolize the two eyes of the tortoise. The northern gate of the city is the tail of the tortoise. It is the lowest spot of the whole city, where all the water in the city flows. There are four barbican entrances in the east and west of the city, facing each other like the paws of the tortoise. This pattern is similar to that of a turtle (the head, tail, and four legs), earning Pingyao the Turtle City. And now we are standing on its tail. Can you point out where we are?

The ancient Chinese people worshipped tortoises, and regarded tortoises as animals of longevity. Because the city gate was used for people to go in and go out, it became the weak point of the security. In order to protect the city, an additional wall was built here. If enemies came, they would be caught just like catching a turtle in a pot. Here you see some weapons used to attack enemies.

The walls measure about 12 meters high, with a perimeter of 6000 meters. A 4-meter wide, 4-meter deep moat can be found just outside the walls. Aside from the four structured towers at the four corners, there are also 72 watchtowers and more than 3000 embrasures. It is said that the 3000 embrasures on the wall represent the number of disciples of Confucius, and the 72 small watchtowers represent his 72 top disciples. The city walls divide Pingyao, a city with an area of around 2.25 square kilometers, into two completely different worlds.

Ok, so much of the Pingyao ancient city wall. You can have a look and take some photos here. Then we'll go on our trip. Thank you for your listening!

Simulated Writing

Directions: Please use the words, phrases or expressions you have learnt to develop a tour commentary according to the Chinese tips, the main contents should include tile, route, extending warm welcome, brief introduction, spot introduction, and conclusion.

女士们，先生们：

早上好！我叫韩梅梅，大家叫我小韩或韩导就行了。首先我代表中国国际旅行社北京分社对您的到来表示最热烈的欢迎！今天我们要游览的景点是故宫，故宫又称紫禁城，是明清两代的皇宫，有24个皇帝在此登基坐殿，统治中国长达500多年。在1924年末代皇帝被逐出故宫后，这里成为了故宫博物院。故宫坐落于北京城的中心，占地72万平方米，有宫殿楼阁9900余间。故宫不但是我国规模最大、保存最完整的古代皇家建筑群，而且还收藏有中国各朝各代的珍贵文物93万余件。故宫红墙黄瓦，金碧辉煌，素有"金色的宫殿之海"的美称。在正式游览之前，我先介绍一下故宫的布局和参观路线。我们眼前的建筑叫午门。午门是紫禁城的正门，俗称五凤楼。清代，皇帝举行朝会或大祀，以及在元旦、冬至、万寿、大婚等重大节日，都要在这里陈设卤簿、仪仗。此外，国家凡有征战凯旋时，皇帝在午门接受献俘典礼，如果皇帝亲征也从午门出驾。请大家跟我来，故宫建筑分为"前朝"和"内庭"两大部分。"前朝"主要由太和殿、中和殿、保和殿组成，统称三大殿，是皇帝发布政会以及举行大典的地方。"内庭"则主要由乾清宫、交泰殿、坤宁宫、御花园及东西六宫组成，是皇帝处理政务和居住享乐的地方。现在我们在外朝的最南端，前面是太和门……

Unit 4　Chinese Ancient Architecture

故宫是我国古代建筑艺术的经典之作，1987年被世界科教文组织列为世界文化遗产，它闪耀着东方文明的光辉！美好的时光总是短暂的，但愿小韩的服务能够让各位领略雄伟壮丽的故宫，接下来给大家半个小时的自由活动时间，请大家拍照和自行游览，谢谢大家！

Part E　Practical Training

Training item 1: Oral Presentation

Directions: You are required to work with your group members to finish the task in this part. Every group should choose a kind of Chinese ancient architecture forms you are familiar to give an introduction. After preparation and practice, a group member will be asked to make an oral presentation; other students may have additional remarks or explanation if necessary. Then teacher may give comments on students' performance.

Training item 2: Role-play

Directions: All the students in the class are divided into several groups, every member in the group choose one role to perform. Students should use the language they have learnt as far as possible.

Situation 1: Ms. Smith, a tourist from USA, comes to Jiangsu province. A local guide Wang Lin is showing him around The Humble Administrator's Garden—a very famous private garden in China. Wang Lin is introducing the knowledge of Chinese gardens like the layout, structure, the feature, and legend, etc.

Situation 2: Ms. Smith is very interested in Qiao's Family Courtyard. A local guide Lily of Shanxi International Travel Service is giving her brief introduction of Chinese residential houses. In addition, Lily offers her more knowledge about other residential houses in China.

Situation 3: Some teenagers from USA will visit Pingyao in Shanxi province next week. You are tour guides from China Shanxi International Travel Service. Please try to write some suitable guide words to introduce Pingyao ancient city walls. Please pay attention to the visitors' age.

Training item 3: Outside-class Work

Directions: Please find some information about other famous imperial palaces or mausoleums in China from books, Internet or some other channels. Try to compare and explain some characteristics of them and then make a brief introduction.

Knowledge links

The Representatives of Chinese Ancient Architectures

China's famous imperial palaces

There are a lot of imperial palaces built in China during the long history. They were splendid and grandiose; unfortunately most of them were destroyed.

Xianyang Palace (咸阳宫), in east of modern Xianyang, Shaanxi province, was the royal palace of the state of Qin. It was urnt down by Xiang Yu after the fall of the Qin Dynasty.

Epang Palace (阿房宫), 15 km west of Xi'an (西安), Shaanxi province, was the fabulous imperial palace built by the First Emperor in replacement of Xianyang Palace. Traditionally said to be burnt down by Xiang Yu, but may not have been completed at the fall of the Qin Dynasty.

Southern Palace (南宫) and **Northern Palace** (北宫), in Luoyang (洛阳), Henan province, was an imperial palace of the Eastern Han Dynasty for two centuries, Demolished by Dong Zhuo at the end of the Han Dynasty.

Daming Palace (大明宫), is now in downtown of Xi'an (西安), Shaanxi province. It is imperial palace of the Tang Dynasty after A.D. 663

Ming Imperial Palace (明故宫), in Nanjing (南京), Jiangsu province, was imperial palace of the Ming Dynasty until 1421. Used as a source of stone and gradually demolished in the Qing Dynasty and by the Taiping rebels.

Forbidden City (紫禁城), is in Beijing, China. It was imperial palace of the Ming Dynasty and Qing Dynasty from 1421 until 1924.

Shenyang Imperial Palace is an emperor museum combining the architectural styles of the minorities of Man, Han and Mongolia. It is the only existing royal palace in China outside the Forbidden City in Beijing.

The sentatives of the imperial gardens

Most of imperial gardens are found in north of China, which are usually spacious, grandiose, and were built for royal families. The representatives are the summer palace, Beihai park, Yuanmingyuan Ruins in Beijing, the Chengde Mountain Resort in Heibei province.

The representatives of the private gardens

Most of the private gardens are found in Suzhou, Jiangsu province, which are usually built in urban areas, neighbored with residences and are generally small in size, but look elegant and tasteful. The representatives are the Humble Administrator's Garden, the Lingering Garden, and the Garden of the Master of Fishing nets.

The representatives of monastic gardens and the gardens in scenic resorts

The representatives of monastic gardens include the Jinci Temple of Shanxi and the Tanzhe Temple of Beijing. The famous scenic gardens are the West Lake of Hangzhou and the Daming Lake of Jinan.

Famous mausoleums

Up to present there have been over one hundred confirmed imperial mausoleums. For examples: The Xiaoling Mausoleum of Emperor Zhu yuanzhang，The Qianling Mausoleum of Emperor Wu Zetian, The Changling Mausoleum of Emperor Zhu Di, The Yuling Mausoleum of Emperor Qianlong and The Dingling Mausoleum of Emperor Wan Li. The

Unit 4　Chinese Ancient Architecture

Mausoleum of Emperor Qin Shihuang was listed as a World Heritage Site by UNESCO in 1987.

The representatives of three types of residential houses in China

The representatives of the northern residential houses include the grand courtyard of Shanxi province, the cave dwelling in some districts in Shaanxi province and dwelling compounds or quadrangles in Beijing; The representatives of the southern residential houses include Hakkas earth building of Fujian province, old village of Sichuan province and Anhui residential houses; The house in minority nationality regions include Yurt in Inner Mongolian Autonomous Region, Diaofang in Tibet Autonomous Region, Ayiwang in Xinjiang Uygur Autonomous Region and Bamboo building of Dai nationality.

Chinese Nationalities and Their Customs

Unit 5

Topic Guidance

There are 56 nationalities in China: the Han majority and the 55 minorities.

Each nationality has developed its unique customs and habits.

China exercises a policy of regional autonomy for various ethnic groups.

Various activities are held during the festivals of different nationalities.

Warming-up

Read the following questions and discuss with your partner.

1. Are there ethnic minorities in the communities you live? How do you communicate with them?

2. Have you ever been invited to be a guest of a minority family? What's your experience?

3. Which part of the minorities' life are you interested in most? Tell us the reason(s).

Look at the following pictures and try to describe it in your own words.

Unit 5 Chinese Nationalities and Their Customs

Part A Listening

Words List

nationality	/ˌnæʃənˈæliti/	n.	民族；国家
reserve	/riˈzəːv/	n.	保护区；保留地；禁猎区
hospitality	/ˌhɔspiˈtæləti/	n.	好客；殷勤
virtue	/ˈvəːtjuː/	n.	美德；优点
minority	/maiˈnɔrəti/	n.	少数民族；少数派
majority	/məˈdʒɔriti/	n.	多数
extremely	/ikˈstriːmli/	adv.	非常；及其
diverse	/daiˈvəːs/	adj.	多种多样的；不同的
custom	/ˈkʌstəm/	n.	习惯；风俗
heritage	/ˈheritidʒ/	n.	遗产；传统
prosperity	/prɔsˈperiti/	n.	繁荣；成功
fundamental	/ˌfʌndəˈmentəl/	adj.	基本的；根本的
objective	/əbˈdʒektiv/	n.	目的；目标
compact	/kəmˈpækt, ˈkɔmpækt/	adj.	紧密的；紧凑的
community	/kəˈmjuːniti/	n.	社区
financial	/faiˈnænʃəl/	adj.	财政的；金融的

Useful Expressions

scenic spot	风景区；景点
historical site	历史遗迹
ethnic group	民族
ethnic minority	少数民族
policy of regional autonomy for ethnic groups	少数民族区域自治政策

Proper douns

the Han nationality	汉族

Activity 1: Spot dictation.

China is country of many (1)_____ and rich cultural reserves. There are many (2)_____ and historical sites all over the 9.6 million square kilometers. Bravery, industry, warmth and hospitality are (3)_____ of the people of each nationality. There are altogether 56 (4)_____ in China. The Han nationality is about 92% of the country's

69

(5)_____. So the other (6)_____ethnic groups are called as the ethnic minorities. These ethnic minorities, together with (7)_____majority, make up the great Chinese nationality known as (8)_____.

These 56 nationalities are extremely diverse. They (9)_____in one or more of the following ways: (10)_____, (11)_____, historical development, (12)_____, and race. Some of the minorities are very similar to the Han, for example, (13)_____ and (14)_____; others are very different. In the long course of historical development, all the nationalities have joined in the effort to (15)_____the great heritage for their (16)_____.

Equality, unity and common prosperity are the fundamental objectives of the (17)_____in handling the relations (18)_____ethnic groups. China exercises a (19)_____ of regional autonomy for various ethnic groups, allowing ethnic groups living in compact communities to (20)_____self-government and (21)_____their own affairs. The central government (22)_____the autonomous areas (23)_____financial and material support to (24)_____the development of the (25)_____economy and culture.

Activity 2: Decide whether the following statements are True or False while listening to the paragraph again.

(   ) 1. In China one can find 56 different nationalities.

(   ) 2. Apart from the Han nationality, the other 55 ethnic groups constitute roughly 8% of the total population.

(   ) 3. The Hui nationality is very different from the Han in many ways.

(   ) 4. Chinese policy officially allows autonomy to the minority nationalities.

(   ) 5. The Chinese central government not only provides the autonomous areas with financial and material support but also direct their affairs.

Activity 3: Choose the correct answer while you are listening.

1. What language do many of the Zhuang nationality speak?
   A. Chinese   B. English   C. Thai
2. What is the Miao minority famous for?
   A. food   B. craftsmanship   C. clothes
3. Who are the forefather of the Hui minority?
   A. Arab and Iranian B. Indian   C. European
4. Which minority are the least concentrated of all the minorities in China?
   A. Menba   B. Miao   C. Manchu
5. Which minority established the Yuan Dynasty in the history?
   A. Manchu   B. Mongolian minority C. Tibetan

Unit 5 Chinese Nationalities and Their Customs

Part B Speaking

Word List

multinational	/ˌmʌltiˈnæʃənəl/	adj	多民族的
distribution	/ˌdistriˈbju:ʃən/	n.	分布；分配
uneven	/ˌʌnˈi:vən/	adj.	不均匀的
territory	/ˈteritəri/	n.	领土；领域
scatter	/ˈskætə/	v.	分散；散开
diversity	/daiˈvə:səti/	n.	多样性；差异
retain	/riˈtein/	v.	保持
costume	/ˈkɔstju:m, kɔˈstju:m/	n.	服装；装束
kimchi	/ˈkimtʃi/	n.	朝鲜泡菜
zanba		n.	糌粑
robe	/rəub/	n.	长袍
embroider	/imˈbrɔidə/	v.	刺绣；镶边
skullcap	/ˈskʌlkæp/	n.	无边便帽
instrument	/ˈinstrumənt/	n.	乐器；仪器

Useful Expressions

on the middle and lower reaches of	在……中下游
roast mutton kebab	烤羊肉串
crusty pancake	馕
sticky rice cake	糯米糕
buttered tea	酥油茶

Proper Nouns

the Yellow River	黄河
the Yangtze River	长江
the Pearl River valley	珠江流域
the Northeast Plain	东北平原
the Hui nationality	回族
the Manchu nationality	满族
the She nationality	畲族
the Uygur nationality	维吾尔族
the Kazak nationality	哈萨克族
the Miao nationality	苗族
the Yi nationality	彝族
the Dai nationality	傣族

71

Korean	朝鲜族；朝鲜人的
Mongolian	蒙古；蒙古人的
Tibetan	藏族；藏族的
the Water Splashing Festival	泼水节
the Torch Light Festival	火把节
the "Eighth of the Fourth Month" Festival	四月八日节
the Nadam Fair	那达慕节
the Antiphonal Singing Day	三月三歌节
the Tibetan New Year	藏历新年
the Spring Festival	春节
the Lantern Festival	元宵节
the Dragon Boat Festival	端午节
the Mid-Autumn Festival	中秋节
the Qingming Festival	清明节
the Double Ninth Festival	重阳节
the PRC	中华人民共和国

Situational dialogue

G: Gao Yang   F: foreign student

F: The Chinese nation is really a multinational country.

G: You are right, sir. The Han nationality is about 92% of the Country's population while the minority nationalities 8% of the population.

F: Ah…The Han nationality makes up the vast majority of the total Chinese population, right?

G: Exactly! But the population distribution is highly uneven. In the large parts of western China the Han nationality is really a minority.

F: That is to say the minorities mainly live in the west, right?

G: Right. The Minority nationalities though only 8% of the population, occupy about 60% of China's territory, mainly distributed in the vast western areas.

F: I see. The minorities are mostly scattered over a vast area.

G: That's true. Do you know the Yunnan province? That's the home to more than 20 ethnic groups. It has the greatest diversity of minority people in China, while the Han people can be found mainly on the middle and lower reaches of the Yellow River, the Yangtze River and the Pearl River valleys, and the Northeast Plain.

F: So how is the different nationalities' life like? Are there some differences?

G: Of course. Because of our country's autonomy policy the minority nationalities have retained their unique customs and habits. All the nationalities are different mainly in language, costumes, food, wedding ceremony, festivals and economical development.

Unit 5 Chinese Nationalities and Their Customs

F: Could you explain them in detail?

G: First, the language is various. Han, Hui, Manchu and She speak Chinese but most of the minorities speak their own languages, some even have written characters.

F: Then what's the difference in food?

G: Generally, people in south China like rice, while people in the north prefer noodles; the Uygur and Kazak nationalities like roast mutton kebab and crusty pancakes; Koreans who mainly live in Jilin Province like sticky rice cakes, cold noodles and kimchi; Tibetans eat zanba and buttered tea.

F: That sounds interesting! How about their costumes?

G: Mongolians wear Mongolian robes and riding boots; Tibetans wear Tibetan robes; Ugyurs wear embroidered skullcaps; Koreans wear boat-shaped rubber overshoes; Miao, Yi and Tibetan women wear gold or silver ornaments.

F: What are the minorities' important festivals? Do they have the traditional festivals?

G: Yes, of course. Each nationality has its own traditional festivals. They include the Water Splashing Festival of the Dai nationality, the Torch Light Festival of the Yi nationality, the "Eighth of the Fourth Month" Festival of the Miao nationality, the Nadam Fair of the Mongolian nationality, the Antiphonal Singing Day of the Zhuang nationality, and the Tibetan New Year of the Tibetan nationality. The most popular festivals among all the nationalities are the Spring Festival, the Lantern Festival, the Dragon Boat Festival, the Mid-Autumn Festival, the Qingming Festival and the Double Ninth Festival.

F: Could you describe the living standard of the minorities?

G: In general, before the founding of the PRC the social and economic development of the minority nationalities is relatively backward compared with the Han people. But with the help of the central government the development of economy, culture, education and medical work in the minority areas has been promoted greatly. In fact, nowadays in most of China's cities and county town, two or more ethnic groups live together.

F: That sounds so encouraging! I'm thinking if I should have a minority customs tour.

G: That's a good idea! You know almost all the ethnic minorities of China are good at singing and dancing, and have unique national musical instruments, beautiful national songs and dances. Now it is just during the Chinese Spring Festival, that's a good chance to have a much better understanding of Chinese nationalities and share their happiness.

F: Ooh…oh, I can't wait to go!

Knowledge improvement

Chinese Ethnic Minority festivals

It is estimated that more than 1200 of the 1700 Chinese festivals are ethnic minorities' festivals. Some of the ethnic minority festivals are so grand and influential that they attract spectators from far away. The following are some of the representative festivals.

Festival	Ethnic Minority	Date
Water-Splashing Festival	Dai	April 14th to 16th
Torch Festival	Yi, Bai, Naxi, etc.	24th to 26th day of the sixth lunar month
Knife-Pole Festival	Lisu	2nd day of the second lunar month
Bullfight Festival	Miao	25th day of the first lunar month
Adult Ceremony	Jino	The day girls turn 15 years old and boys 16 years old
March Fair	Bai, Yi, Hui, Zang, etc	15th to 21st day of the third lunar month
Nadam Fair	Mongolian	July or August
End of Ramadan	Hui, Uygur, Kazak, etc.	The beginning of the tenth month on the Islamic calendar
Corban Festival	Hui, Uygur, Kazak, etc.	The tenth day of the twelfth month on the Islamic calendar

Activity 1: Group discussion.

All the students in the classroom are divided into several groups to discuss which minority you know well and how much you know about them. After discussion, each group chooses a representative to make a presentation, and then the teacher should give the comment on the students' answer.

Activity 2: Make up a dialogue.

Please practice the dialogue for 5 minutes with your deskmates. After that, teacher names some students to choose a role to make up a dialogue and then give comments on their performance if necessary.

Activity 3: Simulated guiding.

All the students in the classroom are divided into several groups and one of the group members acts as a tour guide while others are the tourists from England. Suppose you are on the way to Yunnan province to have a minority customs tour. The tour guide are asked to introduce the general survey of Chinese nationality and give a simple introduction of some minorities. Some phrases and expressions you have learnt may be used in your act.

Part C   Reading

Words List

proclaim	/prəuˈkleim/	v.	宣告；声明
versatile	/ˈvəːsətail/	adj.	多种用途的

Unit 5 Chinese Nationalities and Their Customs

wonton	/ˈwɔnˈtɔn/	n.	馄饨
Timber	/ˈtimbə/	n.	木材；木料
maximum	/ˈmæksiməm/	n.	最大限度；最大量
plough	/plau/	v. / n.	犁地；耕地
mourn	/mɔ:n, məun/	v.	哀悼；忧伤
cemetery	/ˈsemitəri/	n.	墓地
commemorate	/kəˈmeməreit/	v.	纪念；庆祝
symbolize	/ˈsimbəlaiz/	v.	象征
fertile	/ˈfə:tail/	adj.	富饶的；肥沃的
radish	/ˈrædiʃ/	n.	萝卜；小萝卜
kohlrabi	/ˌkəulˈrɑ:bi/	n.	甘蓝；大头菜
hospitable	/hɔˈspitəbl/	adj.	热情友好的
weaving	/ˈwi:viŋ/	n.	编织
brocade	/brəuˈkeid/	n.	织锦；锦缎
handicraft	/ˈhændikrɑ:ft/	n.	手工艺品
sacrifice	/ˈsækrifais/	v. / n.	献祭；祭品
indispensable	/ˌindisˈpensəbl/	adj.	不可缺少的
outfit	/ˈautfit/	n.	用具；全套装备
ancestor	/ˈænsestə/	n.	始祖；祖先
sentimental	/ˌsentiˈmentəl/	adj.	伤感的
lyric	/ˈlirik/	n.	歌词
improvisational	/ˌimprəvaiˈzeiʃənəl/	adj.	即兴的
mosque	/mɔsk/	n.	清真寺
pious	/ˈpaiəs/	adj.	虔诚的；敬神的
veil	/veil/	n.	面纱；面罩
brimless	/ˈbrimlis/	adj.	无边缘的
sanitation	/ˌsæniˈteiʃən/	n.	卫生；卫生设备
feast	/fi:st/	n.	筵席；宴会
permanently	/ˈpə:mənəntli/	adv.	永久的
wail	/weil/	v.	哀号；悲叹
fast	/fɑ:st/	v.	禁食；斋戒
acidic	/əˈsidik/	adj.	酸的；酸性的
elaborate	/iˈlæbərət/	adj.	精心制作的
exquisite	/ˈekskwizit/	adj.	精致的；高雅的
accessory	/əkˈsesəri/	n.	附件；配件
bracelet	/ˈbreislit/	n.	手镯
aesthetic	/i:sˈθetik/	adj.	美的；美学的
totem	/ˈtəutəm/	n.	图腾；崇拜物
ornament	/ˈɔ:nəmənt/	n.	装饰；装饰物
wizard	/ˈwizəd/	n.	术士；男巫
memorial	/miˈmɔ:riəl/	adj.	纪念的；记忆的
substitute	/ˈsʌbstitju:t/	v.	替代；代替

unconstrained	/ˌʌnkənˈstreind/	adj.	不受约束的
martial	/ˈmɑːʃəl/	adj.	战争的；军事的
yurt	/juət/	n.	圆顶帐篷；蒙古包
stockbreeding	/ˈstɔkˌbriːdiŋ/	n.	畜牧业
kumiss	/ˈkuːmis/	n.	马奶酒
ferment	/fəˈment/	v.	发酵；(使)发酵
auspice	/ˈɔːspis/	n.	吉兆
niche	/nitʃ/	n.	壁龛
archery	/ˈɑːtʃəri/	n.	箭术
trotter	/ˈtrɔtə/	n.	猪；羊蹄
intestine	/inˈtestin/	n.	肠子；肠
acupuncture	/ˈækjuˌpʌŋktʃə/	n.	针灸；针刺
massage	/ˈmæsɑːʒ/	n.	按摩；揉
etiquette	/ˈetiket/	n.	礼节；礼仪
burial	/ˈberiəl/	n.	葬礼；埋葬
prohibition	/ˌprəuhiˈbiʃən/	n.	禁止；禁令

Useful Expressions

be composed of	由……组成
burst into laughter	突然大笑
be reputed as	被称为
descend from	起源于；由……传下来
see off	送行；送别
drive out	驱赶
weigh up	估量；称
ward off	避开；挡住
drink up	喝完
propose a toast	敬酒；举杯
staple food	主食；主粮
glutinous rice dumpling	粽子
lunar calendar	阴历
animal husbandry	畜牧业
process industry	加工工业；制造工业

Proper Nouns

the Qin Dynasty	秦朝
the Warring State Period	战国时期
Guangxi Zhuang Autonomous Region	广西壮族自治区
the Devil festival	中元节；鬼节
the Valentine's Day	情人节

Unit 5　Chinese Nationalities and Their Customs

Arabic	阿拉伯人的
Persian	波斯；波斯人的
Muslim	穆斯林
Muhammad	穆罕默德
Lesser Bairam	开斋节
Corban festival	古尔邦节
the Inner Mongolian Autonomous Region	内蒙古自治区
UNESCO	联合国教科文组织
the Tibetan Autonomous Region	西藏自治区
the Tibetan Plateau	青藏高原

Customs of Different Nationalities in China

As a large united multi-national state, China is composed of 56 ethnic groups. Each nationality has its own unique customs and habits of life developed in the process of its long history.

Customs of the Han nationality

As the largest ethnic group in both China and world wide, the Han people live mainly on agriculture, and made outstanding achievements in the fields of politics, philosophy, art, literature and natural science.

Confucianism, Taoism and Buddhism, are the main religions of the Han people.

The Han people worship the tiger and dragon. Ever since the Qin Dynasty in the third century B.C. all the emperors in Chinese history proclaimed themselves "the son of the dragon". The tiger, on the other hand, has always belonged to the people. People love its beauty and strength, and use it as a protector and symbol of good luck.　Many kinds of tiger objects can be found in the house of the Han people: a tiger head made of cloth hanging on the gate, tiger papercuts on the window, tiger pillows and quilts on the bed, a tiger cake on the table and tiger caps, shoes and toys for children.

The staple food of Han is rice and wheat. Rice is versatile and can be served in a variety of ways including porridge, rice cake, glutinous rice dumpling and rice noodles. Wheat is used in the production of steamed bread, noodles, steamed stuffed buns and wonton. Han people living in different regions of China have formed unique styles of cooking. The eight cuisines are the representative. Tea and alcohol are the Chinese traditional drinks. The Han Chinese likes to entertain their honored guests with Chinese tea and alcoholic drinks.

House styles and materials of the Han people vary in different regions of China. Those built in North China are mostly made of bricks in the courtyard style. The courtyard in Beijing is a representative. For houses in Northeast China, the style is almost the same as that in North China except for the walls. As Northeastern China is extremely cold, walls are built thicker and more solid than those of other places to retain warmth. However, in southern China, the Han people build their houses mainly of timber. All the houses of Han are suggested to be positioned in the north facing south to catch the maximum sunlight.

The Spring festival, also known as the Lunar New Year or the Chinese New Year is the most important and exciting festival in China. It usually falls in late January or early February. The historical reason for beginning the year during cold winter is that it is the time after the autumn harvest and winter storage, the time before "spring ploughing and summer weeding". In other words, this is a time for rest and relaxation after a year's hard work.

The Lantern festival (also called Yuanxiao festival) is on the 15th day of the first Chinese lunar month. Yuan literally means first, while Xiao refers to night. Yuanxiao is the first time when we see the full moon in the new year. Since there is an exhibition of lanterns on that night, it is called the Lantern Festival. Other amusement at the festival include firework displays and dances. Another important part of the festival is eating small dumpling balls made of glutinous rice flour.

Qingming Festival, meaning clear and bright, is the day for mourning the dead, so this festival is a combination of sadness and happiness. It falls in early April every year. After the festival, the temperature will rise and rainfall increase. It is high time for spring ploughing and sowing. On the Qingming Festival, all cemeteries are crowded with people who came to sweep tombs and offer sacrifices.

The Dragon Boat Festival or Duanwu Festival falls on the fifth day of the fifth month of the Chinese lunar calendar. This festival is widely accepted as a day to commemorate Qu Yuan, China's greatest poet of the Warring State Period (475B.C.—221B.C.). For thousands of years, Duanwu Festival has been marked by eating Zongzi and racing dragon boats. So Duanwu Festival is also known as the Dragon Boat Festival.

The Mid-Autumn Festival falls on the 15th day of the eighth lunar month because the eighth lunar month is mid-autumn and the fifteenth is the middle of that month. On that night the moon is supposed to be brighter and fuller than any other night. In China, a full moon is round and symbolizes reunion, this festival is also known as the festival of reunion.

Customs of the Zhuang nationality

Of China's 55 minority ethnic groups, the Zhuang ethnic minority is the largest one with a long history and glorious culture. Over 90% of the Zhuang people live in Guangxi Zhuang Autonomous Region so the region is known as the "home of the Zhuang".

Most Zhuang people live in waterside areas in the plain, with fertile land, plentiful rain and rich resources. The crops go ripe twice or three times a year. It is suitable for the growing of glutinous rice and other paddy rice.

The Zhuang people are good at making glutinous food. And they have the habit of making pickles, including sour cabbage, sour bamboo shoots, salty radish and kohlrabi, etc. They love hunting and cooking wild animals and eating insects. They eat all kinds of meat, including beef, mutton, pork and chicken, etc. Before meals, they will take a little from

Unit 5 Chinese Nationalities and Their Customs

each dish and let the dog eat first. The Zhuang people are so hospitable that any guests are honored by the whole village. Wine is a must when treating the guests. The elder person is shown respect by nobody eating before him or her.

The Zhuang women are skilled at weaving and embroidering. Zhuang brocade is a splendid handicraft which originated in the Tang Dynasty (618—907). The brocade is excellent for making quilt covers, table-clothes and handbags. Now Zhuang brocade is not only a wonderful handicraft favored by the people in China but also has won international fame and enjoys a large market abroad.

The bronze drum used both in sacrifice and festivals, delivers a special culture of the Zhuang ethnic minority. On the top and sides of the drums, the sun, frogs, dancing human figures with wings, and boat racing, dragon and other patterns are decorated. These reflect the Zhuang people's traditional culture. They worship the sun, believe in the Frog Goddess and beat copper drums when they celebrate festivals, and hold boat races. Nowadays, the bronze drum has become an indispensable musical instrument for the festivals.

Besides sharing similar festivals with the Han, the Zhuang minority has its unique ones.

The Devil Festival is held on July 14th of the lunar month. The day before the Devil Festival, every family does a thorough house cleaning and makes special preparations of outfits used in the sacrifice. On that day, duck, pork and good wines along with some candies and fruits must be offered in order to show great respect to their ancestors.

The Singing Festival is a traditional occasion which was held to visit graves of the ancestors. Now it has become a grand sentimental occasion using songs for their expression. On that day, after sacrificing Sanjie Liu (a Zhuang minority girl good at singing), the Zhuang people will sing to each other to challenge each other not only the song itself but also wit. Lyrics are usually improvisational and humorous that makes every one burst into laughter. It is also a perfect day for the young men to express their love to the girls by singing, so it is also reputed as the Valentine's Day of the Zhuang ethnic minority.

Customs of the Hui minority

The Hui are one of the largest among China's ethnic minorities, they are descended from the Arabic and Persian merchants who came to China during the 7th century. According to historical records, they came to China and settled, intermarried with the local people, built mosques and formed a new ethnic—the Hui. The majority of the Hui group live in the Ningxia Hui Autonomous Region.

The Hui are pious Muslims. They pay great attention to personal sanitation. They pray 5 times a day and each time they wash themselves before praying. They use a specially made aluminum kettle for washing.

The clothes of the Hui are also influenced by their religion: Men wear white caps and women veils. The color of the veil reflects the owners' status: unmarried young women wear pink or other veils; middle-aged women wear black ones, and those over 60 wear white veils.

Men, except for clerks and elders who wear yellow or white silk caps, mostly wear white brimless cloth caps.

The Hui eat mutton and beef. A whole roast sheep and hotpot are their favorite dishes. Hui are generally forbidden to eat the meat of pigs, dogs, horses, donkeys, mules as well as the blood of animals. Visiting guests will be served a wide variety of distinctive food and fruits or home-made cakes and will receive infused tea. All the family members will come to greet their guests, and even will be seen off out of the Hui people's village.

The living customs differ from the other ethnic groups. For example, marriage outside the Hui group is not encouraged. For the marriage feast, there are usually 8 to 12 dishes. The even number of dishes is important as it symbolizes that the new couple will be a pair permanently. Funerals of Hui people are simple, but they do not wail, as that will be regarded as the complaint or hatred for the dead. They do not like to joke nor do they describe things with food. Smoking, drinking and gambling are frowned upon and young people are not permitted to sit with the elder members of the group. Use of a fortune teller to predict the future is prohibited. They avoid sitting or stepping on any threshold, for it is said Muhammad used the threshold as his pillow.

During the entire ninth month of to the Hui calendar, men older than 12 and women older than 9 will fast, which means they cannot eat anything from sunrise to sunset. Lesser Bairam is celebrated on the first day of the tenth month and lasts three days. Relatives and friends are served choice beef and mutton, and fired cakes which are their favorite food.

Corban Festival is on the tenth day of the last month. The morning of the festival, they do not eat breakfast. After attending the mosque, they kill oxen and then share them with the poor families and relatives. Selling of the oxen is not permitted on this day.

Customs of the Miao nationality

The Miao ethnic minority is larger than most of minority groups in China. They live mainly in Guizhou, Yunnan, Hunan, Hubei, Hainan provinces and the Guangxi Zhuang Autonomous Region.

The staple food of the Miao ethnic minority is rice. Other dishes are meat and acidic soups. Pickled vegetables, hot seasonings and home-made wine are common at the table. Glutinous rice becomes a must during festivals and celebrations.

The Miao are known for elaborate embroidery and exquisite work with silver. All girls there can embroider. Once a girl was born, her mother would try her best to teach her identifying different colors. By the time the girl could use needle and thread, her mother would teach her to embroider, because a girl who can't embroider well, no mater how beautiful she is, won't attract guys' attention.

Silver accessories are a standard for the Miao people. For more than 400 years, it's been the custom to decorate oneself head to toe with silver. They include silver hat, silver horns, silver comb, silver ear-rings, neckband, necklace, bracelet, etc. A full set can weigh up to

Unit 5 Chinese Nationalities and Their Customs

10kg. The purpose of wearing all this silver is on the one hand for aesthetic function, on the other hand to ward off evil and as symbols of wealth. The Miao nationality's clothes bear strong cultural message. The patterns range from ancient totem to historic legend. Historians view it as the "Wearable History Book". Most of the silver accessories are made by hands in a traditional way. A silver head-piece takes a couple of months to finish. In some villages, every male is trained in silver-work. Each ornament is an exquisite work of art and sparkles with the wisdom of the Miao people. It is a tradition that, when a girl is born, her parents will start saving money to make and collect fancy silver ornaments that can weigh several kilograms. And on the wedding day, the girl will be wearing these beautiful silver accessories, adding joyful atmosphere to the happy event.

The Miao people believe that everything in nature has a spirit, which in combination are mighty enough to control their lives. Every time there are disasters, they will invite a wizard to perform ceremonies designed to drive out the devil ghost. They worship their ancestors so much that memorial ceremonies are very grand. Sacrifices such as wine, meat, and glutinous rice are costly.

Miao's New Year is an annual event where the Miao people celebrate the great harvest of the past year. The Miao people spread widely areas, so there are various way of celebrating this holiday. Most of time, this holiday falls in September, October or November. To the Miao people, this festival is on the same level as the traditional Chinese New Year.

With the influence of the Han Chinese, Miao began to substitute this holiday with the Chinese New Year. However, traditions and customs remained. At this holiday, dancing, singing and horseracing will be seen. In addtion, it is a time for young goys and girls to meet.

Customs of the Mongolian nationality

The Mongols (also called Mongolian) ethnic minority is distributed primarily in the Inner Mongolian Autonomous Region. This ethnic minority is brave and unconstrained with a profound history. Though they called themselves "Mongol", meaning everlasting fire, other people refer to them as "an ethnic minority on the horseback". They enjoy music and poetry, and much of their culture relates to their past martial glory.

A written language was created in the 13th Century, and Mongolian scholars have written texts on history, language, literature, medicine, astronomy and weapons. The Mongolians have made brilliant achievements in their literature. The "Mongolian Secret History" has been listed among the world's famous works by UNESCO.

Most Mongolian live in the countryside. Many engage in animal husbandry and live in traditional "yurts" or round tents. Stockbreeding plays a major role in their development, together with agriculture, handicrafts and other processing industries.

The Mongolian people take meat and milk as their daily staple food and drink. They enjoy drinking the milk of sheep, horses, deer and camels. Kumiss, fermented out of horse milk, is a kind of distinctive wine with the function of driving out coldness and as well as strengthening the stomach. Tender, boiled mutton, "Shouzhua Rou" in Chinese, is representative of their traditional food. These people were so skilled in their cooking that they were able to cut the meat into pieces without chopsticks.

The Mongolians are unconstrained and warm-hearted people as they treat others warmly and politely. They greet everyone they meet during their travels even they do not know each other. To present hada which represents holy and auspice, and to hang it onto the guest's neck means that they consider their guests are very distinguished. The guests should bend forward as a way to express their gratitude.

When visit the Mongolian the guests should not dry their feet or boots on the stove, nor should they wash or bathe in the river, as it is holy and clean in their eyes. Besides the guests should not step on the threshold, sit beside the niche of Buddha, and touch children's heads.

The grandest festival is the Nadam Fair for 5-7 days during late August. Mongolian people, in new clothes, will gather from many areas. Many will participate in the exciting competitions of horseracing, archery, wrestling, as well as song and dance.

Customs of the Tibetan nationality

The Zang ethnic minority (also known as Tibetan) mainly live in the Tibetan Autonomous Region on the Tibetan Plateau. The Zang people are famous for expressing their feelings through song and dance, notably the step dance and the masked Tibetan opera.

Tibetans have food of a very distinctive character. Among the great variety of Tibetan food, zanba and buttered tea are the most popular and distinguished. Other typical Tibetan foods include dried meat, mutton served with sheep's trotters, roast sheep intestine, yogurt and cheese.

Tibetan medicine, combining various forms of traditional Chinese medicine, is said to have developed the schools of acupuncture and massage. It has been enjoying an increase in fame due to its somehow magical effect on some hard-to-cure diseases.

Presenting hada is a common practice among the Tibetan people to express their best wishes on many occasions, such as wedding ceremonies, festivals, visiting the elders and the betters and entertaining guests. The white hada, a long narrow scarf made of silk, embodies purity and good fortune. When you come to a Tibetan family, the host will propose a toast, usually barley wine. You should sip 3 and then drink up. To entertain guests with tea is a daily etiquette. The guest has not to drink until the host presents the tea to you. Sky burial is a common form in Tibet. There are many prohibitions. Strangers are not allowed to attend the ceremony.

The most important festival is the Tibetan New Year. They clean their rooms in preparation for that day, paint symbols of auspice, and warmly greet each other in the morning.

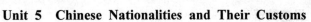

Unit 5 Chinese Nationalities and Their Customs

Activity 1: Choose the correct answer to complete the following sentences.

1. The _____ people worship the tiger and dragon.
   A. Manchu   B. Mongolian   C. Han

2. The Zhuang _____ not only is very famous in China but also enjoys a large market abroad.
   A. bronze drum   B. brocade   C. Silver accessory

3. _____ is the Hui nationality's important festival.
   A. Lesser Bairam   B. The Nadam Fair   C. The Singing Festival

4. The _____ of Miao nationality is viewed as the "Wearable History Book".
   A. veil   B. clothes   C. hada

5. _____ is representative of the Mongolian traditional food that can be cut into pieces without chopsticks.
   A. Kumiss   B. zanba   C. Shouzhua Rou

6. Sky burial is a common form in _____.
   A. Guangxi   B. Tibet   C. Inner Mongolia

Activity 2: Fill in the table according to what you have learnt.

Nationality	Distribution	Food	Drink	Festivals
Han				
Zhuang				
Hui				
Miao				
Mongolian				
Tibetan				

Activity 3: Answer the following open questions.

1. Do you know other festivals of different nationalities besides those mentioned in the text? What are they?

2. Have you ever tried the food of the minorities? Are you used to it?

3. Can you introduce briefly one or two of the Ethnic Minority Tours?

Part D   Writing

Compose Tips and Instructions

旅游期间的注意事项是提醒游客在旅游目的地逗留期间应避免去做的事情。一般包括以下几方面：人身安全、钱物保管、证件存放安全、饮食卫生注意事项、风俗禁忌注意事项、突发事件预防等。措辞要言简意赅，为了让游客能有一个安全愉快的旅行，做好提醒工作是十分必要的。注意事项一般由标题、正文以及感谢、祝愿等内容构成。

Sample

Situation： A tour group from America is about to visit the Huangshan Mountain, Miss Liu, a local guide from Huangshan Sunshine Holiday Travel Agency, will give the tourists some tips and instructions before they set out.

Tips and Instructions

(1) Please take good care of your personal ID card, tickets and other valuables when leaving the hotel.

(2) It is advised that suitcases and excess luggage be deposited at the hotel. Just bring an overnight bag to the top of the mountain. A backpack is easier to carry.

(3) Wear a pair of good climbing shoes when climbing the mountain. And Don't forget to bring enough warm clothes and waterproofs. Don't wear skirts.

(4) Carry water or other drinks to prevent dehydration and snacks to keep your energy levels up. The prices are more expensive at the scenic spots.

(5) Watch your footing when climbing the steps and be mindful of your safety when taking photos.

(6) There is no smoking allowed on the mountain, except in the smoking areas.

(7) If there is a storm, please do not climb to the summits or stand under trees which may be struck by lightning.

(8) Use a raincoat for protection from the wind and rain. Don't use an umbrella as it can be an inconvenience or even a hazard.

(9) Please keep away from monkeys at the scenic spot. Don't bring out food in front of them.

Unit 5 Chinese Nationalities and Their Customs

(10) Those who have asthma, high blood pressure, heart problems or other health conditions please bring along enough medicine and water in case of emergency.

(11) Don't travel alone. Those to whom mountain climbing presents a serious health risk are recommended to take the cable cars and sedan chairs.

(12) Tourists should follow tour guides' suggestions and instructions. Don't ignore good advice or else problems and accidents may occur.

Thank you so much!

May you have a splendid journey!

Simulated Writing

Directions: Please use the words, phrases or expressions you have learnt to write tips and instructions according to the Chinese presentation.

注意事项

(1) 请您携带并保管好个人身份证、机票等，离开房间时要锁好门。

(2) 请您根据自己的身体状况带一些必备的药品，如：感冒药、晕车药等。

(3) 乘车、乘船不要争抢拥挤。

(4) 注意饮食卫生，多吃绿叶蔬菜、水果，多喝水。

(5) 吃海鲜后，一小时内不要食用冷饮、西瓜等。

(6) 餐后不宜马上去游泳。

(7) 景区食物价格较高，游客可携带一些方便食品在船上食用。

(8) 游泳前要作好准备活动。游泳时请在规定区域内，当感到不适时要马上上岸休息。

(9) 携带儿童的游客应照顾好自己的孩子，不要让他们自由活动。

多谢合作！

祝大家旅途愉快！

Part E Practical Training

Training item 1: Oral Presentation

Directions: You are required to work with your group members to finish the task in this part. Every group should choose an ethnic group you are familiar with and give an introduction. After preparation and practice, a group member will be asked to make an oral presentation, other students may have additional remarks or explanation if necessary. And then the teacher gives comments on the students' performance.

Training item 2: Role-play

Directions: All the students in the class are divided into several groups, every member in the group choose one role to perform. Students should use the language they have learnt as far as possible.

Situation 1: The Brown, tourists from USA, comes to Yunnan province, the home to more than 20 ethnic groups. A local guide Lily is introducing the local ethnic minorities and their customs like the different food, costumes, interesting lifestyles etc.

Situation 2: Mr. Brown together with his friends is very interested in the prairie of the Inner Mongolia and the "ethnic minority on the horseback"——the Mongolian nationality, and a local guide Lily is giving him brief introduction of the customs of this ethnic group, like their traditional food and drink, lifestyle, festivities and even some etiquette when they entertain their guests.

Situation 3: Lily, a local guide from China Hainan International Travel Service, is giving the tourists from England some tips and instructions before they leave the hotel for Yalong Bay.

Training item 3: Outside-class Work

Directions: Please find some information about other ethnic minorities in China from books, Internet or some other channels. Try to compare and explain some characteristics of them and then make a brief introduction.

Knowledge links

Holidays in China

Chinese people legally enjoy over 115 days off including 104 days of weekends and 11 days of festivals. The table below provides detailed information of Chinese 7 legal holidays in a year.

Festival	Date	Legal Holidays
New Year's Day	Jan. 1	1 day
Spring Festival	subject to the lunation	3 days
Qingming Festival	Apr. 4 or 5	1 day
May Day	May 1	1 day
Dragon Boat Festival	the 5th day of the 5th lunar month	1 day
Mid-Autumn Day	the 15th day of the eighth lunar month	1 day
National Day	Oct. 1	3 days (Oct. 1~3)

Traditional Sports and Activities

With a long history China have developed several unique and traditional sports and

Unit 5 Chinese Nationalities and Their Customs

pastimes. Some are practiced widely by the Han minority, while some are popular in the minority groups.

Horse Racing (Saima)

The main contests involve racing, horsemanship to demonstrate the handling of the mount as well as the ability of the animal achieved through its training, shooting and throwing spears while in the saddle and picking up "hada"; these are silk favors and an auspicious symbols of esteem for the rider.

Dragon Boat Racing (Sai Longzhou)

Many ethnic groups in the southern China and Han People have continued the custom of the Dragon Boat Racing for the Dragon Boat Festival. The Zhuang, Miao, Dai, Bai and Tujia people decorate the boats to resemble a dragon and shout their support with drums and gongs. Craftsmen exercise their skills to the full with their carving and painting to decorate each boat.

Stepping on High (Gaoqiao)

In Hunnan province the Miao and Tujia ethnic groups are very fond of a sport called "gaoqiao" which means "stepping on high". They made short stilts from bamboo poles about 1-meter-high (3.3 feet). These would be strapped to their legs and what was a useful way of getting around has been developed into a skill and in traditional games people not only walk on these stilts but they run at speed demonstrating great feats of agility and balance. This is similar to the performance of "stepping on high" in festivals of the Han People.

Mongolian Wrestling (Shuaijiao)

A sport loved by the Mongolian people. The winner will finally be declared the wrestling hero. Besides the wonderful game itself, the dress of wrestlers is also a distinctive highlight.

Lion Dance (Wushi)

It brings joy to occasions such as the Spring Festival, Lantern Festival, wedding celebrations and opening ceremonies for businesses and so on. For this dance, there are two types of lion—those of the north of the Yangtze River and those of Southern China. The northern lions are vivid with golden hair. By contrast most Southern lions look quite fierce.

Chinese Cuisine

Unit 6

Topic Guidance

Chinese cuisine has a long history, and is one of the Chinese cultural treasures.

Chinese cookery is characterized by fine selection of ingredients, precise processing, particular care to the amount of fire and substantial nourishment.

Local flavors, snacks and special dishes have formed according to regions, local products, climate, historical factors, and eating habits.

Warming-up

Read the following questions and discuss with your partner.

1. How much do you know about the Chinese cuisine?
2. What kind of famous dishes does your city have?
3. Can you name some of local cuisines? And what characteristics do they have?

Look at the following pictures and try to describe it in your own words.

Unit 6 Chinese Cuisine

Part A Listening

Words List

cuisine	/kwɪˈziːn/	n.	烹饪艺术；菜肴
harmonious	/hɑːˈməʊniːəs/	adj.	和谐的；和睦的；协调的
integration	/ˌɪntɪˈɡreɪʃən/	n.	结合；整合；一体化
aroma	/əˈrəʊmə/	n.	芳香；香味；气味
fineness	/ˈfaɪnnəs/	n.	精致；纤细；细微；优雅；良好
instrument	/ˈɪnstrumənt/	n.	器具；仪器；器械；乐器
seasoning	/ˈsiːzənɪŋ/	n.	调味品；调味料；佐料
employ	/ɪmˈplɔɪ/	v.	雇用；使用；利用
unparalleled	/ʌnˈpærəleld/	adj.	无比的；无双的；空前的
complicated	/ˈkɒmplɪkeɪtɪd/	adj.	结构复杂的
stew	/stjuː/	v.	炖；煨
braise	/breɪz/	v.	炖；焖
simmer	/ˈsɪmə(r)/	v.	炖；慢煮
ultimately	/ˈʌltɪmətli/	adv.	最终；最基本地；根本上
savor	/ˈseɪvə/	v.	品尝；欣赏
determine	/dɪˈtɜːmɪn/	v.	决心；决定
partake	/pɑːˈteɪk/	v.	吃；喝
distinctive	/dɪˈstɪŋktɪv/	adj.	有特色的；与众不同的
amazing	/əˈmeɪzɪŋ/	adj.	令人惊异的
dexterity	/dekˈsterəti/	n.	技巧；技能

Useful Expressions

hand down	把……传下去；传给(后代)
aspire to	渴望；追求
in itself	本质上；就其本身而言
at table	在进餐；在进餐时；在餐桌边
living habits	生活习惯
harmonious integration	和谐统一

Activity 1: Spot dictation.

Cuisine in China is a (1)_____ of (2)_____, shape and the fineness of the instruments. For the cooking process, chefs pick various (3)_____ while employing unparalleled complicated skills (4)_____ from their fathers, ever(5)_____ their ideal of perfection for all the senses. Among the many cooking methods they use are boiling,

(6)_____, braising, (7)_____, steaming, (8)_____, baking, and (9) and so on. When they finish their (10)_____ they are arranged on a variety of plates and dishes so that they are a real pleasure to view, to smell and ultimately to (11)_____. The facility to partake of these delights is also distinctive – (12)_____! To see even the smallest child eat with such (13)_____ is quite amazing for many foreigners. The use of two simple sticks in this way is an art (14)_____ and chopsticks (15)_____ the way in which Chinese food is presented at table.

Since China has (16)_____, and the produce, climate and (17)_____ are quite different in each place, the flavor of food is quite different: southerners like light food, northerners prefer (18)_____, Sichuan people like (19)_____, Shanxi people like sour food and so on. China has all kinds of cuisine of special local flavor, among which that of Shandong, Sichuan, Jiangsu, Guangdong, Zhejiang, Fujian, Hunan and Anhui are all quite (20)_____.

Activity 2: Decide whether the following statements are True or False while listening to the paragraph again.

(   ) 1. Cuisine in China is a harmonious integration of color, aroma, taste, shape and the fineness of the instruments.

(   ) 2. The cooking process employs very easy skills handed down from their fathers.

(   ) 3. The facility to partake of these delights is also distinctive——chopsticks, which is quite amazing for many foreigners.

(   ) 4. The southerners like a heavily seasoned taste, northerners prefer light food.

(   ) 5. China has many kinds of cuisine according to different regions.

Activity 3: Choose the correct answer while you are listening.

1. When the chopsticks were invented?
   A. in the spring
   B. in the autumn
   C. in the Spring and Autumn Period

2. What does the man mean?
   A. He is from Sichuan.
   B. He like Sichuan Cuisine.
   C. He doesn't mention what he likes.

3. How is Chinese medicinal cuisine made from?
   A. Chinese medicinal cuisine is made from food.
   B. Chinese medicinal cuisine is made from medicine.
   C. Chinese medicinal cuisine is made from food and medicinal ingredients following the theory of Chinese medicine.

Unit 6 Chinese Cuisine

4. Why most Chinese women are slim and men free of cardiovascular diseases?
   A. Because Chinese women and men don't like eating vegetables.
   B. Because the main ingredients of Chinese cuisine is vegetables.
   C. Because Chinese women and men like doing exercises.
5. Why Chinese people like something round?
   A. The round table, round dishes and round bowls all symbolize union and perfection.
   B. Things like round table, round dishes and round bowls look very nice.
   C. It reflects the Chinese nation of division.

Part B Speaking

Words List

itinerary	/aiˈtinərəri/	n.	旅程；行程
slaughter	/ˈslɔːtə(r)/	v.	屠杀；杀戮；屠宰
wafer	/ˈweifə/	n.	薄片；薄脆饼
smear	/smiə/	v.	涂抹
sauce	/sɔːs/	n.	调味汁；酱汁
cylinder	/ˈsilində/	n.	圆筒；圆柱；圆柱体
slicing	/ˈslaisiŋ/	n.	切片
yummy	/ˈjʌmi/	adj.	美味的
knowledgeable	/ˈnɔlidʒəbəl/	adj.	博学的；有见识的；知识渊博的

Useful Expressions

get hooked	着迷的
fore-feeding	硬喂，填鸭式
mouth-watering	令人垂涎的，流口水的
roll…into	把……卷成
Bon Appétit	(法语)祝胃口好

Proper Nouns

Beijing Roast Duck	北京烤鸭
Quanjude Restaurant	全聚德饭店
Qianmen	前门大街是北京著名商业街。位于京城中轴线，北起前门月亮湾，南至天桥路口，与天桥南大街相连

Situational dialogue 1

After visiting the Forbidden City, Mr. Brown, a visitor from USA together with Lily, a local guide, is going to taste some Chinese famous dishes. They are talking about Chinese dishes.

B: Brown   L: Lily

B: I've just heard Chinese food is well-known and has a variety of dishes. There are Sichuan Cuisine, Shandong Cuisine, Cantonese Cuisine and Shanghai food etc.

L: Yes. Each type of food has its particular flavor and is cooked in special ways. Today we can try something unique.

B: I'm just interested. I prefer to enjoy the beautiful scenery of China with the local delicacies. Since I'm visiting Beijing, surely I'd try something particular in Beijing.

L: Beijing Roast Duck has the reputation of being the most delicious food Beijing has to offer. Some find it a bit too greasy, but others get hooked after one taste. In any case, a Beijing Roast Duck dinner is usually a fixed item on any Beijing tour itinerary. Eating Beijing Roast Duck is also one of the two things you are absolutely supposed to do while in Beijing. The other one is climbing the Great Wall.

B: Enjoying the Chinese scenery, tasting the Chinese food and appreciating the Chinese culture are my great joy of this trip. Where shall we go to taste the Beijing Roast Duck?

L: Quanjude Restaurant of Qianmen is famous for Beijing Roast Dusk.

B: Can you tell me something about the dish?

L: A duck is fore-feeding before it is slaughtered. When roasting, the duck is filled with water until the roasting is done and then the duck is hooked on a spit in a huge, round oven. The best roasted duck is date-red, shining with oil, but with a crisp skin and tender meat. The chef then cuts the meat into thin slices, each having a piece of skin. Then the meat is served with very thin pancakes, spring onions and special sauce.

B: I'm mouth-watering.

(At Quanjude, Mr. Brown is sampling the culinary creation of Beijingers. Lily is explaining the right way to eat this delicacy.)

L: First hold a wafer pancake in your left hand, and then pick up two or three pieces of meat with the slivered spring onions, or leeks. Don't forget to smear some sauce in the middle of the pancake.

B: Like this?

L: Great. Then roll the pancake into a cylinder shape, fold over the lower end so that the sauce does not spill out.

B: Could you tell me something about this restaurant?

L: The restaurant has a history about 130 years. Its unique art of roasting ducks earned it an excellent reputation both at home and abroad. The wood of fruit trees such as date, peach and pear are used in the roasting process to add the meat a distinctive aroma. The slicing of the duck meat is an art itself. How do you like it?

B: It's so yummy. And you are so knowledgeable! Cheers for your hard work!

L: Thank you! Bon Appétit!

Unit 6 Chinese Cuisine

Knowledge Improvement

Table Manners

The main difference between Chinese and Western eating habits is that unlike the West, where everyone has their own plate of food, in China the dishes are placed on the table and everybody shares. If you are being treated by a Chinese host, be prepared for a ton of food. Chinese are very proud of their culture of food and will do their best to give you a taste of many different types of cuisine. Among friends, they will just order enough for the people there. If they are taking somebody out for dinner and the relationship is polite to semi-polite, then they will usually order one more dish than the number of guests (e.g. 4people, 5dishes). If it is a business dinner or a very formal occasion, there is likely to be a huge amount of food that will be impossible to finish.

A typical meal starts with some cold dishes, like boiled peanuts and smashed cucumber with garlic. These are followed by the main courses, hot meat and vegetable dishes. Finally soup is brought out, which is followed by the starchy "staple" food, which is usually rice or noodles or sometimes dumplings. Many Chinese eat rice (or noodles or whatever) last, but if you like to have your rice together with other dishes, you should say so early on.

One thing to be aware of is that when eating with a Chinese host, you may find that the person is using their chopsticks to put food in your bowl or plate. This is a sign of politeness. The appropriate thing to do would be to eat the whatever-it-is and say how yummy it is. If you feel uncomfortable with this, you can just say a polite thank you and leave the food there, and maybe cover it up with a little rice when they are not looking. There is a certain amount of leniency involved when dealing with Westerners, so you won't be chastised.

Activity 1: Group discussion.

All the students in the classroom are divided into several groups to discuss the Beijing Roast Duck, including the roasting process, the way of eating and the restaurant—Quanjude. After discussion, each group chooses a representative to make a presentation, and then the teacher should give the comment on the students' answer.

Activity 2: Make up a dialogue.

Please practice the dialogue for 5 minutes with your partner. After that, teacher names some students to choose a role to make up a dialogue and then give comments on their performance if necessary.

Activity 3: Simulated guiding.

All the students in the classroom are divided into several groups, and every group member may try to act as a local guide in class to simulate a situation of introducing a local delicacy. Some phrases and expressions you have learnt may be used in your commentary.

Part C　Reading

Words List

region	/ˈriːdʒən/	n.	地区；区域
virtuosity	/ˌvəːtʃuˈɔsəti/	n.	高超技艺；精湛演技
diversity	/daiˈvəːsəti/	n.	多样性；多样化
genre	/ˈʒɑːnrə/	n.	类型；流派
essential	/iˈsenʃl/	adj.	必不可少的；根本的
alien	/ˈeiliən/	adj.	陌生的；不熟悉的
aquatic	/əˈkwætik/	adj.	水生的；水栖的
proximity	/prɔkˈsiməti/	n.	接近；附近
melon	/ˈmelən/	n.	瓜；甜瓜
mellow	/ˈmeləu/	adj.	醇香
abalone	/ˌæbəˈləuni/	n.	〈美〉鲍鱼(软体动物)
savory	/ˈseivəri/	adj.	美味的；可口的
exterior	/eksˈtiəriə/	n.adj.	外面；外表；外部的
interior	/inˈtiəriə/	n.adj.	内部；里面；内部的
sea cucumber	/siː ˈkjuːkʌmbə/	n.	海参
asparagus	/əˈspærəgəs/	n.	芦笋；芦笋的茎；龙须菜
prawn	/prɔːn/	n.	对虾；大虾；明虾
inclusion	/inˈkluːʒən/	n.	包括；包含
numb	/nʌm/	adj.	麻木的；失去知觉的
cayenne	/keiˈen/	n.	红辣椒
auxiliary	/ɔːgˈziliəri/	adj.	辅助的；备用的
mince	/mins/	n. v.	切碎；剁碎；绞碎
pock-marked	/pɔk mɑːkt/	adj.	有麻子的
ingenious	/inˈdʒiːnjəs/	adj.	灵巧的；善于创造发明的
sheet	/ʃiːt/	n.	薄板；薄片
translucent	/trænsˈluːsənt/	adj.	半透明的
slippery	/ˈslipəri/	adj.	滑的；滑得抓不住的
reddish	/ˈrediʃ/	adj.	淡红色的；微红的
tingling	/ˈtiŋliŋ/	n.	发麻；麻刺感；麻感
embody	/imˈbɔdi/	v.	表现；象征；包括；包含
dense	/dens/	adj.	稠密的；浓密的
morsel	/ˈmɔːsəl/	n.	少量；分成小块
cobra	/ˈkəubrə/	n.	眼镜蛇
grimalkin	/griˈmælkin/	n.	猫；老母猫；恶毒的老妇
pullet	/ˈpulit/	n.	(尤其指不到一年的)小母鸡

Unit 6 Chinese Cuisine

elaborately	/iˈlæbəreitli/	adv.	精心制作地；精心地
contend	/kənˈtend/	v.	争夺；竞争；声称；主张
famed	/feimd/	adj.	著名的；出名的
chrysanthemum	/kriˈsænθəməm/	n.	菊花；小雏菊
meticulously	/meˈtikjuləsli/	adv.	极细心地；一丝不苟地
enumerate	/iˈnuːməˌreit/	v.	列举；枚举；数
breadth	/bredθ/	n.	宽度
concubine	/ˈkɔŋkjəˌbain/	n.	妾；妃子
mussel	/ˈmʌsl/	n.	贻贝；蚌类
seduce	/siˈdjuːs/	v.	诱使堕落；使入迷
aromatic	/ˌærəˈmætik/	adj.	芳香的；有香味的
greasy	/ˈgriːsiː/	adj.	脂肪的；含脂肪过多的
interlink	/ˌintə(ː)ˈliŋk/	n. v.	连结；连环
fowl	/faul/	n.	鸟；禽；家禽；鸡 禽肉
enhance	/inˈhɑːns/	v.	提高；增加；加强
shrimp	/ʃrimp/	n.	虾；小虾
metaphor	/ˈmetəfə/	n.	隐喻
conglomeration	/kɔnˌglɔməˈreiʃən/	n.	团块；聚集；混合物
resembles	/riˈzembl/		像；类似于
delicate	/ˈdelikit/	adj.	柔和的；清淡可口的；清香的
marinade	/ˌmæriˈneid/	n.	腌泡汁
recipe	/ˈresəpi/	n.	烹饪法；食谱；方法；秘诀；诀窍
fin	/fin/	n.	鱼鳍
litchi	/ˈliːtʃiː/	n.	荔枝；荔枝树
longan	/ˈlɔŋgən/	n.	龙眼
medlar	/ˈmedlə/	n.	欧楂；欧楂属植物；欧楂果
constitution	/ˌkɔnstiˈtjuːʃən/	n.	构成方式；构造；宪法
eye-catching	/ˈaiˌkætʃiŋ/	adj.	令人注意的
nutritious	/nuːˈtriʃəs/	adj.	有营养的；营养丰富的；滋养的
inspired	/inˈspaiəd/	adj.	有创造力的
tempting	/ˈtemptiŋ/	adj.	吸引人的；诱人的
grilled	/grild/	adj.	烤的；有格子的；炙过的

Useful Expressions

compare to	与……比较
be originated from	源自于……
be particular about	在……有特色，特别
red-fermented-rice	红糟
have a far-reaching influence on	对……具有深远的影响
have a high reputation in the world	在世界上具有极高的声誉

Proper Nouns

Eight Cuisine	八大菜系 (Shandong Cuisine, Sichuan Cuisine, Guangdong Cuisine, Fujian Cuisine, Jiangsu Cuisine, Zhejiang Cuisine, Hunan Cuisine and Anhui Cuisine)
Qi	齐国[Qi state]。中国周朝分封的诸候国名(公元前1122年—公元前265年)，在今山东省。
Lu	鲁国[Lu state]。中国春秋时国名,在山东省南部。周武王封其弟周公旦于鲁。战国时为楚所灭。
Ba	巴。古国名，在今中国四川省东部。泛指四川：～蜀。～山蜀水。
Shu	蜀。中国周代诸侯国名，在今四川省成都市一带。
the Qin dynasty	秦。朝代名(公元前221年—公元前206年)，是由周朝的秦国(在今陕西甘肃一带)统一全中国后建立的中国历史上第一个中央集权的朝代。

Braised abalone　　红烧鲍鱼
Sweet and Sour Carp　　糖醋鲤鱼
Eight Immortals Crossing Sea Teasing Arhats　　八仙过海闹罗汉
Stir-fried tofu with minced beef in spicy been sauce—Ma Po Tofu　　麻婆豆腐
Lamp-shadow beef　　灯影牛肉
Lung pieces by the couple　　夫妻肺片
Gong bao ji ding　　宫爆鸡丁
Chrysanthemum fish　　菊花鱼
Braised snake porridge　　烩蛇粥
Roast suckling pig　　烤乳猪
Fried golden bamboo shoot with chicken mince　　鸡茸金丝笋
Buddha jumping over the wall　　佛跳墙
Dongbi dragon pearl　　东壁龙珠
Fried Xi Shi's tongue　　炒西施舌
Three sets of ducks　　三套鸭
Boiled dry thread of Tofu　　大煮干丝
Lion's head braised with crab-power　　清炖蟹粉狮子头
West-lake braised fish in vinegar　　西湖醋鱼
Shelled shrimps cooked in Longjing tea　　龙井虾仁
Stewed fins　　红煨鱼翅
Immortal chicken with five elements　　五元神仙鸡
Braised turtle with ham　　火腿炖甲鱼
Fuliji Grilled chicken　　符离集烧鸡

Unit 6 Chinese Cuisine

Chinese Cuisine

Chinese cuisine is a general term of the dishes of each region and each ethnic group in China. It has the following characteristics: long history, virtuosity of cooking, diversity of cooking methods and ingredients, and its special styles. Chinese cuisine has experienced a few thousands years of development, and now it has a high reputation in the world. Chinese cooking is also an important part of Chinese culture, and has a far-reaching influence on the East-Asian region.

Chinese cuisine is particular about its color, fragrance, flavor, meaning and form. Therefore, compare to the dishes of other countries, the Chinese dishes are more colorful, exquisite and harmonious.

Chinese cuisine has a number of different genres, but the most influential and typical known by the public are the "Eight Cuisine". These are as follows: Shandong Cuisine, Sichuan Cuisine, Guangdong Cuisine, Fujian Cuisine, Jiangsu Cuisine, Zhejiang Cuisine, Hunan Cuisine and Anhui Cuisine. The essential factors that establish the form of a genre are complex and include history, cooking features, geography, climate, resources and life styles. Cuisines from different regions are so distinctive that sometimes despite the fact that two areas are geographical neighbors their styles are completely alien.

Shandong Cuisine was originated from the ancient state of Qi and Lu in what is today's Shandong province in China, formed in Qin Dynasty. It is a local flavor cuisine which has the most extensive coverage in China throughout Peking, Tianjin and Tanggu region and Northeast China.

Major characteristics of Shandong Cuisine.

(1) Prepared with a wide variety of materials. For example, Jiaodong dishes are mainly made of aquatic products due to its proximity to the Yellow Sea. People in Jinan like to prepare cuisine with mountain delicacies and seafood delights, melons, fruits, vegetables and peppers.

(2) A pure, strong and mellow taste, rather than a mixed taste. Chefs excel at using shallots and garlic.

(3) Shandong Cuisine is known for its excellent seafood dishes and delicious soup.

(4) Chefs are good at preparing clear, smell, crisp, tender and delicious dishes by frying, stirring and steaming.

The typical menu can include many delicate dishes such as Braised Abalone—smooth, delicate, fresh and savory. Sweet and Sour Carp—with crisp exterior and tender fish interior, a little sweet and sour.

Eight Immortals Crossing Sea Teasing Arhats—This is a starter before a celebration feast. It is luxurious and traditionally uses its eight main ingredients: fin, sea cucumber, abalone, asparagus, prawns and ham. The stock is flavored and the Arhats are symbolized by the inclusion of chicken breast.

Sichuan Cuisine was originated from the ancient state of Shu and Ba in what is today's Sichuan province in China, and formed approximately between the union of China in Qin Dynasty by the Emperor Qin and the Three Kingdoms period. Sichuan Cuisine is characterized by its numb and spicy, fresh and fragrance. In addition, cayenne pepper, Sichuan pepper and pepper are most important auxiliary material when cooking Sichuan dishes. Therefore, it formed its unique flavor and now the cuisine is very popular in China.

The main-characteristics of Sichuan Cuisine.

(1) Prepared with a wide variety of ingredients.

(2) Presenting various shapes and tastes, and famous for spicy food, fish-flavored shredded pork and food with odd taste.

(3) Boasting numerous cooking techniques, such as stir frying, frying, stir-frying before stewing and braising.

Delicious dishes:

Stir-fried tofu with minced beef in spicy been sauce—a real feast of tender bean curd, minced beef, pepper and bean sauce. It is said that it was made by a pock-marked but ingenious woman, hence the name Ma Po Tofu (pock-marked woman's bean curd).

Lamp-shadow beef—the beef is cut in very thin sheet. When a piece is carried, it looks like translucent paper, slippery and reddish. When put under the lamp or light, a red shadow will appear.

Lung pieces by the couple—a quite popular in Chengdu. It got the name because the dish was ever sold by a couple and today it remains the original savor, tender meat, tingling and spicy.

Gong bao ji ding—this is a tender chicken dish, tender as the meat is quickly fried. Flavored with peanuts, this is tasty and very popular.

Guangdong Cuisine is one of the main cuisine styles in China, formed in Qin Dynasty, is composed of Guangzhou, Chaozhou and Dongjiang cuisine. It is famous in its fresh and lively cooking ingredients, delicious taste, beautiful color and wide-varieties, and has a high reputation in China as well as the world.

(1) An important feature is that the flavor of Cantonese cuisine is always changing according to the seasons. In summer and autumn the flavor is lighter however in winter and spring is stronger.

(2) Guangdong Cuisine features sour, bitter, spicy and delicious tastes with a clear and fragrant smell.

(3) Guangdong snacks are peculiar about ingredients, some sweet and some salty.

There is an old saying: "Guangdong serves best food in the country". Now we can say: "Guangdong offers delicacies from all over the world".

Typical menu here can embody these following characteristics.

Chrysanthemum fish—chefs with adept cutting techniques shape the fish like

Unit 6 Chinese Cuisine

chrysanthemums, each individual morsel being convenient to enjoy with either chopsticks or forks.

Braised snake porridge—of rare meat of cobra, grimalkin and pullet, braised elaborately, also called "Dragon and tiger contending" (Long Hu Dou).

Roast suckling pig—a famed dish with rather long history, golden and crisp exterior and tender meat inside, with dense aroma.

Fujian Cuisine was originated in Minhou county, Fujian province. It is famous for its red-fermented-rice seasoning and sweet-sour taste, specialized in soup-making.

Fujian Cuisine has the following characteristics.

(1) Chefs are skilled in the use of a kitchen knife, full of interest.

(2) The Fujian people are peculiar about soup, which is full of changes.

(3) A wide variety of seasonings are used, with unique characteristics.

(4) Clear, refreshing, delicious and light tastes, slightly sweet and sour.

Appealing dishes are countless, so we can only enumerate some of them.

Fried golden bamboo shoot with chicken mince—every 100g of winter bamboo shoots will be cut into 500~600 strips with same length and breadth. Then they can blend with the very small pieces of chicken.

Buddha jumping over the wall—the most famous and classical dish, which has a long history since the Qing Dynasty.

Dongbi dragon pearl—it chooses materials from the rare longyan tree of thousands year's history in Kaiyuan Temple in Quanzhou, the delicate scent is rather catching.

"Fried Xi Shi's tongue" is made from the locally produced Fujian mussel. According to the legend of the concubine, Xishi, of the king of the state of Wu was thrown in the sea tied to a huge stone by wife of Gou Jian, the king of Yue who destroyed Wu, to prevent her husband being seduced by her beauty. In the area of the sea where she sank, a special bread of mussel appeared and this was said to be Xi Shi's tongue.

Jiangsu Cuisine was very popular in China during Qing Dynasty. Usually it tastes light and moderate.

The main characteristics of Jiangsu Cuisine.

(1) Distinguished for exquisite ingredients, freshness and aliveness.

(2) High cutting techniques.

(3) Have a good command of duration and degree of heating and cooking.

(4) Good at keeping the original taste one particular taste for one dish. All dishes have light, mellow and refreshing tastes. Yangzhou Cuisine is light and elegant; Suzhou Cuisine is slightly sweet; and Wuxi Cuisine is fairly sweet.

(5) Pay great attention to soup, which is strong but not greasy and delicious.

The most highly recommended courses are.

Three sets of ducks—an interlinking dish, that is to put pigeon into wild duck, then put the wild dusk into a fowl duck. When stewed, the fowl duck is tender, the wild one crisp, and the little pigeon delicate!

Boiled dry thread of Tofu—thanks to the exquisite skills of chefs, the tofu can be cut into very thin threads which have chances to absorb the savor of soup. When chicken pieces added to the soup, the dish is called "chicken dry thread"; likewise, when shrimp added, it makes "shrimp dry thread".

Lion's head braised with crab-power—there is a metaphor in the dish name. In actual fact the lion's head is a conglomeration of meat that is shaped like a sunflower and resembles a lion's head. It can be braised in a clear soup, or be re-cooked in a dense soup. A seasoning of crab powder enhances the flavor.

Zhejiang Cuisine was formed in Zhejiang province. Normally it is in a refined compact shape and tastes soft and moderate. Of a large number local cuisine styles, Zhejiang Cuisine occupies an important position and mainly consists of Hangzhou, Ningbo, Shaoxing and Wenzhou cuisine styles, each having its own local characteristics.

(1) Hangzhou Cuisine, the representative of Zhejiang Cuisine, is delicious, light, crisp, elegant and highly finished.

(2) Ningbo local dishes are delicious, tender, soft and refreshing.

(3) Shaoxing Cuisine, which has the characteristics of the kind of fish, includes various kinds of local dishes, which are soft and aromatic with original soup, light oil, and a heavy taste. Chefs are forbidden to use peppers.

(4) Wenzhou Cuisine is known for delicious seafood and light and delicious dishes.

West-lake braised fish in vinegar—a traditional delicacy in Hangzhou. It is said that there was once a boy who made his living by fishing. When he fell ill, his sister-in-law fished for him and braised the fish she caught with a marinade of vinegar and sugar. He was said to have made an immediate recovery after eating it. The boy's story aroused the attention of the emperor and the recipe has been used ever since.

Shelled shrimps cooked in Longjing tea—as the Longjing tea is taken as the best tea in Hangzhou, which is reputed for greenness, fragrance, pure taste and elegant looks, when the living shrimps are stir-fried in the Longjing, the dish sends a refreshing aroma and is quite delicious.

Hunan Cuisine has been already formed in Han Dynasty. It is in a mountain-area style and normally it tastes sour and spicy.

Hunan Cuisine has three characteristics.

(1) Skillful use of a kitchen knife, a delicious taste and a beautiful shape.

(2) Known for sour and spicy dishes by adding various kinds of seasonings.

(3) Adopting a wide variety of techniques.

Stewed fins—it had been famous during the Qing Dynasty. Choice fins, chickens, pork are stewed in chicken soup and sauce, tasting really fresh and mellow.

Unit 6 Chinese Cuisine

Immortal chicken with 5 elements—a dish made by putting 5 elements, litchi, longan, red dates, lotus seeds and medlar, into the body of a chicken, then to braise. The taste is rather peculiar and it is said to have the effect of strengthening the constitution.

Anhui Cuisine was originated in Huizhou, usually the cooking materials are collected in the mountain-area and the dishes are in heavy oil and dark color.

Anhui Cuisine has the following four characteristics.

(1) Using a wide variety of ingredients.

(2) Adopting unique techniques.

(3) Paying great attention to nutritious food.

(4) Offering various kinds of dishes, some of which are full of local flavor.

Among these delicacies, some of the traditional ones are eye-catching.

Braised turtle with ham—the oldest dish using the special "Mati turtle" The delightful taste of this dish has inspired poets.

Fuliji Grilled chicken—the cooking technique was derived from Dezhou braised chicken of Shandong province, with improvement of the technique by chefs at Fuliji. The grilled chicken is golden and tempting, and the meat is so well cooked that it falls easily from the bone.

There are also other delicious cuisines such as Beijing Cuisine, Dongbei Cuisine, Uygur Cuisine and Hubei Cuisine. As the capital of China, Beijing always offers a vast variety of dishes from all over the country. Consequently, no matter where you visit, there will be fascinating food that you can enjoy.

Activity 1: Choose the correct answer to complete the following sentences.

1. According to the text, Chinese cuisine can be divided into _____ types
   A. 8   B. 6   C. 4

2. The essential factors to form the Chinese cuisine are _____ .
   A. history, cooking features, geography
   B. climate, resources and life styles
   C. all above

3. Generally speaking, Shandong Cuisine has _____ ; while Sichuan Cuisine is characterized by its _____ .
   A. numb and spicy; a pure and strong taste
   B. a pure and strong taste; numb and spicy
   C. slight and strong; pure and spicy

4. _____ is one of the main cuisine styles in China. It is famous in its fresh and lively cooking ingredients, delicious taste, beautiful color and wide-varieties.
   A. Guangdong Cuisine   B. Sichuan Cuisine   C. Zhejiang Cuisine

5. Dongpo Pork is one of famous dishes in _____.
   A. Anhui Cuisine   B. Hunan Cuisine   C. Zhejiang Cuisine

Activity 2: Fill in the table according to what you have learnt.

Chinese Cuisine	Time for Origin	Related Areas	Cooking Features	Famous Dishes
Shandong Cuisine				
Sichuan Cuisine				
Guangdong Cuisine				
Fujian Cuisine				
Jiangsu Cuisine				
Zhejiang Cuisine				
Hunan Cuisine				
Anhui Cuisine				

Activity 3: Answer the following open questions in brief.

1. Do you know any other famous dishes? What are they?
2. Have you ever tasted any dishes of Beijing Cuisine? What features does it have?
3. Can you tell some difference between Sichuan Cuisine and Anhui Cuisine?
4. Can you introduce some dishes or snacks from your hometown?
5. Which types do you like best of Chinese cuisine? Why?

Part D　Writing

An Introduction to a Local Cuisine
撰写地方风味简介

地方风味是吸引游客的亮点之一，是游客在欣赏名胜美景之外的物质和精神上的的又一享受。因此，在对旅游景点作宣传的同时，让游客更多的了解各地方风味，品尝更多样的地方佳肴也是旅游服务的关键。

撰写地方风味一般包括以下几点：

(1) 菜名。中文菜名常常美化之作用的原料、烹饪的方法和做出来的成品的视觉效果。

(2) 特色。每种地方风味能够流传至今，与其独特的风味特色息息相关。

(3) 原料。不同的菜肴用料不一，要适当介绍烧制原料，加深客人对菜肴的了解。

(4) 起源。与菜肴有关的掌故、传说能让一道菜更具文化内涵与历史意义。

(5) 烹饪方法。菜肴的烹调方法在中国文化中占有很重要的一部分，堪称一绝。

(6) 地位。说明该菜肴在中国主要菜系中的地位或其当今受欢迎的程度。

Unit 6 Chinese Cuisine

(7) 食用方法。一些特殊菜肴食用时方法一定要正确，这样才能让用膳者有最好的享受。

(8) 注意事项。有些菜肴食用会引起用膳者的某些不适，要提前给予说明。

另外，在撰写地方风味时，尽可能使用通俗易懂的语言，采用读者喜闻乐见的形式。在介绍其文化内涵时，注意掌握语言的跨心理、跨交际性特点。

Sample

Situation： A tour group from America arrive at Tianfu Restaurant. Miss Zhang Qing, a local guide from China Chengdu International Travel Service, is introducing the local cuisine of Sichuan Hot-pot.

Sichuan Hot-pot

Ladies and gentlemen:

Welcome to Tianfu Restaurant. Today what we will taste is the famous Sichuan Hot-pot.

Legend has it that it was first developed by Sichuan people beggars, who deposited all the culinary alms that they received during winter into a bubbling pot. The mouth-watering aroma attracted passers-by then it was wide spread.

The Sichuan Hot-pot tastes very spicy. The broth is flavored with chili peppers and other pungent herbs and spices. The main ingredients include hot pepper, Chinese prickly ash, thick broad-bean sauce, ginger grain, beef fat, crystal sugar and wine. Slices of kidney, chicken breast, beef tripe, goose intestines, spring onion, soya bean sprouts, mushroom eel, duck and sea cucumber form the meat content of the dish.

The cooking takes only 8～10 seconds. This way of coking helps to preserve the taste of the food and the vitamins.

And for those who like to cool their palate after the chili shock, many Sichuan restaurants now serve a Hot pot that is divided into two sections—one containing a spicy broth, the other a milder white stock.

Simulated Writing

Directions: Please use the words, phrases or expressions you have learnt to write an introduction to a local cuisine according to the Chinese tips.

过桥米线

(Cross-bridge Rice Noodle)

过桥米线是云南特有的名小吃，它不仅是一道美食，也是云南的历史、饮食、人文的缩影。

过桥米线始创于清乾隆年间,至今已有 200 多年的历史。它的发明制作还有这样一段广为流传的故事。乾隆年间,云南红河蒙自有一王姓书生,为准备考试便到蒙自南湖的湖中小岛上看书,她的妻子每天都要给他送饭菜,但由于路途遥远,等到王秀才吃饭时,佳肴早已变得冷冰冰的。某日,其妻杀鸡熬汤为其补身,孰料秀才忙于苦读,忘了食用。傍晚时分,其妻再次送来晚饭时,发现鸡汤仍未食用本想责备秀才一番,可手碰到土罐时却发现土罐中的鸡汤居然还很烫,揭盖一看,原来是汤面上厚厚的鸡油封住汤面,所以使得汤持久不冷。其妻受到启发,回家一试,滚热的鸡汤还可以将米线、蔬菜、肉片等烫熟食用。自此,王秀才每天便可吃到热腾腾、香喷喷的米线了。由于其妻每天送饭要过桥,所以,此米线做法流传开后,人们就将它命名为过桥米线。

过桥米线最考究的还是它的汤,如果汤不好,它配置的辅菜再好也是枉然。它的汤必须用纯正肥土鸡为主要材料,同时附上筒子骨、上等火腿用小火慢慢熬,直至汤色清澈透亮、香气扑鼻,鸡油随滚滚沸汤翻滚如十月盛开的金菊时方可。

下面再说说配料,过桥米线自然少不了米线,过桥米线一般选用干浆米线,因为米线要在汤中烫熟了吃,如果用酸浆米线时间烫长了米线的酸味就会溢出来破坏汤的味道。其他的配料分为肉和蔬菜两类。蔬菜讲究时鲜,一般这时节有什么蔬菜就用什么蔬菜。肉类,则讲究刀工,即切片。过桥米线的肉片都薄如蝉翼,这样才能确保肉片下汤即熟。

最后说说过桥米线别具一格的吃法。过桥米线的汤都是滚汤,但是由于上面有厚厚的鸡油所以汤不会冒热气,乍眼一看还以为是碗冷汤。所以吃的时候一定不要被表面现象所迷惑,贸然喝汤。应当先下配料,下料次序是先下肉类,再下蔬菜,最后下米线。过几分钟,过桥米线的汤便会将这些生料烫熟,这时一碗营养丰富,黄白相间,香飘四溢的过桥米线就可以吃了。

Part E Practical Training

Training item 1: Oral Presentation

Directions: You are required to work with your group members to finish the task in this part. Every group should choose one of the Chinese cuisine you are familiar to give an introduction. After preparation and practice, a group member will be asked to make an oral presentation; other students may have additional remarks or explanation if necessary. And then the teacher gives comments on the students' performance.

Training item 2: Role-play

Directions: All the students in the class are divided into several groups, every member in the group choose one role to perform. Students should use the language they have learnt as far as possible.

Unit 6　Chinese Cuisine

Situation 1: Mr. White, a visitor from USA, comes to Shandong province. He is very interested in Shandong Cuisine. He decides to Qi-Lu Grand restaurant to have a taste. A local guide Sherry is accompanying with him. Sherry is introducing the features of Shandong Cuisine and some famous dishes.

Situation 2: Mr. White is walking along the gourmet street with his local Guide Li Ping. Li Ping is introducing the Sichuan famous Snacks to Mr. White while tasting them.

Situation 3: Cantonese Cuisine attracts foreigners from all over the world. After a week's of visiting and tasting, Mr. Brown, a foreigner from England, is telling out his unforgettable feelings.

Training item 3: Outside-class Work

Directions: Please collect all kinds of information about Chinese food culture as possible as you can. Try to understand them, share them with you classmates, finally make a brief introduction.

Knowledge links

Chinese Medical Cuisine

Chinese medicinal cuisine is a long standing tradition. Early records show that it was in use as far back as the Han Dynasty (206 B.C.—220 B.C.). Through continual improvement during the succeeding dynasties, it has developed into a practical science of nutrition. This is not a simple combination of food and traditional medicine, but it is a distinctive cuisine made from food and medicinal ingredients following the theory of Chinese medicine.

This not only became the means of health-preservation among the people of China, but also spread abroad, especially popular in Southeast Asia. There is a wide choice of foods that are used in many different ways to promote heath. It is estimated that there are more than 600 different kinds of resources ranging from creeds, fruits, vegetables, meats and marine products. Many of these will be unfamiliar to foreigners; however all are quite precious and effective in the field of medicinal food. Many different ingredients are used to add to the appeal as well as to strengthen effects of cuisine. Wine, sugar, oil, salt, vinegar and honey, and other commonly used items such as almonds, mandarin orange or peanuts, all are utilized in the cooking process.

According to its respective functions, medicinal cuisine is classified under four categories: health-protection dishes, prevention dishes, healing dishes and therapeutic dishes.

Health-protection dishes refer to reinforcement of required nutritional food correspondingly to maintain the organic health. A soup of pumpkin and almond can help lose weight; soup of angelica and carp can add beauty; and ginseng congee can give more strength.

Prevention dishes build resistance to potential ailments. "Mung bean soup" is considered helpful as a guard against heat stroke in summer. Lotus seeds, lily, yam, chestnuts and pears can assist in the prevention of dryness in autumn and a strengthening of resistance to cold in winter.

Healing dishes are the medicinal food for rehabilitation after severe illness. "Broiled sheep's heart with rose" or "braised mutton with angelica" will help to rebuild a healthy constitution.

Therapeutic dishes aim at the specific pathology. "Fried potatoes with vinegar" can adjust the organ and restrain hypertension and carp soup with Tuckahoe may enrich the strength of blood plasma albumen to help reduce swelling.

China's Local Specialties

Unit 7

Topic Guidance

China has various exquisite ancient vessels made of pottery, porcelain and bronze.

China is a country with a rich variety of handicrafts such as shadow puppets, paper cuts and so on.

There are three major kinds of brocade and four kinds of embroidery in China.

Warming-up

Read the following questions and discuss with your partner.

1. Can you name some ancient Chinese containers used for holding food and wine?
2. Do you know how to make a kite?
3. How much do you know about the "Silk Road"? What are the three major kinds of brocade and four famous kinds of embroidery?

Look at the following pictures and try to describe it in your own words.

Part A　Listening

Words List

splendid	/ˈsplendid/	adj.	非常好的；华丽的
heritage	/ˈheritidʒ/	n.	遗产
vessel	/ˈvesl/	n.	容器；器皿
bronze	/brɒnz/	n.	青铜；青铜艺术品
incense	/ˈinsens/	n.	香（尤指宗教礼仪用的）
pottery	/ˈpɒtəri/	n.	陶器；制陶技艺
porcelain	/ˈpɔːsəlin/	n.	瓷；瓷器
polish	/ˈpɒliʃ/	v.	擦亮；修改
sheen	/ʃiːn/	n.	光泽
terracotta	/ˌterəˈkɒtə/	n.	赤陶土；赤陶
zenith	/ˈzeniθ/	n.	天顶；鼎盛时期
texture	/ˈtekstʃə(r)/	n.	质地；手感
decorative	/ˈdekərətiv/	adj.	装饰性的；作装饰用的
celadon	/ˈselədɒn/	n.	青瓷
dominant	/ˈdɒminənt/	adj.	首要的；占支配地位的
treasure	/ˈtreʒə(r)/	n.	珠宝；财富
ornamentation	/ˌɔːnəmenˈteiʃn/	n.	装饰；点缀
inscription	/inˈskripʃən/	n.	刻印文字；题词
usher	/ˈʌʃə(r)/	v.	引导；引领

Useful Expressions

in the form of	以……的形式
have a history of	有……的历史
at its best	处在最好状态
lie in	在于……
musical instrument	乐器
home of pottery and porcelain	陶瓷发源地
tri-coloured pottery	三彩陶

Proper Nouns

Longshan Culture	龙山文化
Bronze Age	青铜器时代

Unit 7 China's Local Specialties

Activity 1: Spot dictation.

China has splendid (1)_____ in the long history. Various vessels, made of (2)_____, bronze and other materials are important ones. They were made (3)_____ all kinds of items, such as bowls, cups, (4)_____, vases, jewel cases, incense burners, (5)_____ and so on. Pottery and porcelain have a history of more than 8000 years in China. The word "china" clearly shows that the country is the "home of pottery and porcelain." The black pottery of the (6)_____ was (7)_____ a fine sheen. Terracotta was at its best in the Qing Dynasty, and tri-colored pottery (8)_____ at the time of Tang Dynasty. The earliest porcelain ware was found in the Shang Dynasty. The features of porcelain lie in texture of basic body, color of glaze, (9)_____, shape and style Celadon (like the color of jade) and black porcelain wares were the (10)_____ at Han Dynasty. The porcelain wares of the Song Dynasty are considered classics. The bronze wares were unique (11)_____ for China (12)_____ for their impressive designs, classical decorative ornamentation, and (13)_____. The Shang and Zhou Dynasties ushered China into the height of the (14)_____. Bronze can (15)_____ four main types based on function: food vessels, (16)_____, water vessels and musical instruments. In ancient China the making of bronze ware (17)_____ the imperial families and aristocrats. And the possession of such wares was regarded as a status symbol. (18)_____ counterparts in other parts of the world, the Chinese bronze ware (19)_____ their inscriptions which are regarded as major chapters in the Chinese (20)_____.

Activity 2: Decide whether the following statements are True or False while listening to the paragraph again.

(   ) 1. Many kinds of household containers became culture heritages in China.

(   ) 2. Pottery and porcelain have a history of less than 8000 years in China.

(   ) 3. The features of porcelain lie in texture of basic body, color of glaze, decorative pattern, shape and style.

(   ) 4. The porcelain wares of the Tang Dynasty are considered classics.

(   ) 5. Bronze can be classified into three main types based on function.

Activity 3: Choose the correct answer while you are listening.

1. Which place is called the Porcelain Capital?
   A. Jingdezhen   B. Wuyuan   C. Nanjing

2. When did porcelain wares become common?
   A. In the Shang Dynasty.

B. In the Han Dynasty.

C. In the Tang Dynasty.

3. What are ritual vessels?

A. Ritual vessels are bronze wares for daily use.

B. Ritual vessels are bronze wares used for sacrificing.

C. Ritual vessels are bronze wares for recreation.

4. Which is not true about Simuwu Ding?

A. It is the largest existing bronze ware in the world.

B. It was a symbol of imperial power.

C. It was cast in the Han Dynasty.

5. What does Tom mean?

A. Peter should choose tea ware according to the color of tea.

B. Peter should choose tea ware according to the price of tea.

C. Peter should choose tea ware according to the flavor of tea.

Part B   Speaking

Words List

sculpture	/ˈskʌlptʃə(r)/	n.	雕像；雕刻品
folklore	/ˈfəʊklɔː(r)/	n.	民俗；民间传说
audience	/ˈɔːdiəns/	n.	观众；听众
lingering	/ˈlɪŋgərɪŋ/	adj.	缠绵的；缓慢消失的
exquisite	/ɪkˈskwɪzɪt/	adj.	精美的；微妙的
brisk	/brɪsk/	adj.	清新的；敏捷的
hallway	/ˈhɔːlweɪ/	n.	通道；走廊
framing	/ˈfreɪmɪŋ/	n.	框架
distinctive	/dɪˈstɪŋktɪv/	adj.	独特的；有特色的
handicraft	/ˈhændikrɑːft/	n.	手工艺品
engrave	/ɪnˈgreɪv/	v.	雕刻
flexibility	/ˌfleksəˈbɪlɪti/	n.	适应性；灵活性
hesitation	/ˌhezɪˈteɪʃn/	n.	踌躇；犹豫
waggle	/ˈwæɡl/	v.	摆动；扭动
longevity	/lɒnˈdʒevəti/	n.	长寿
celebration	/ˌselɪˈbreɪʃn/	n.	庆典
entertainment	/ˌentəˈteɪnmənt/	n.	娱乐；娱乐片
innovation	/ˌɪnəˈveɪʃn/	n.	创造；新思想

Unit 7 China's Local Specialties

cloisonné	/klwɑːˈzɔneɪ/	n.	景泰蓝瓷器
combination	/ˌkɔmbiˈneɪʃn/	n.	结合；结合体
mold	/mɔld/	v.	塑造；铸模
dazzle	/ˈdæzl/	v.	使目眩，使眼花
utensil	/juːˈtensl/	n.	器皿；家什
bracelet	/ˈbreɪslət/	n.	手镯；手链

Useful Expressions

originate from	源于
be abundant in	富有
shadow puppet	皮影
Chinese knot	中国结

Proper Nouns

| China Shaanxi International Travel Service | 中国陕西国际旅行社 |

Situational dialogue 1

A local guide Chen Jing from China Shaanxi International Travel Service is showing guests from Australia around Shu Yuan Men (The Arts Street)—a well-known street in the style of ancient towns in Xian. Various crafts and arts are sold on this crowded street all year long.

T: tourists   G: local guide

G: Ladies and gentlemen, now what we are going to visit is the well-known Arts Street. It's very crowded here. Please take good care of your pockets.

T: The buildings along the street look so old. Do they have a very long history Miss Chen?

G: Absolutely. The buildings were rebuilt according to the Ming and Qing styles. This area was the cultural center of Xi'an at that time.

T: Oh, what's this?

G: They are shadow puppets. They were first made of paper sculpture, later from the hides of donkeys or oxen. That's why the Chinese name for shadow puppet is pi ying, which means shadows of hides. Shadow puppetry was very popular during the Tang and Song Dynasties in many parts of China.

T: What are they used for?

G: Well, these are traditionally used in telling folk stories. Besides the figures needed in a certain drama, the shadow puppets include heroes from folklore and history, such as the four ancient beauties, Xi Shi, Wang Zhaojun, Diao Chan, and Yang Guifei ; or the Monkey King, Emperor Qin Shi Huang. Shadow puppetry wins the heart of an audience by its lingering music, exquisite sculpture, brisk color and lively performance.

111

T: That sounds very interesting. I even want to watch a performance.

G: Ok, if there is time you can. Now walk down and you will approach a hallway on your right. Mall artists sell paintings, paper cuts, scrolls and silk paintings. Some are farmer's paintings and created in local style. This would be a treasured gift and framing is available and reasonable.

T: Miss Chen, are these paper cuts?

G: That's right. Paper-cut is a very distinctive visual art of Chinese handicrafts. It originated from the 6th century when women used to paste golden and silver foil cuttings onto their hair at the temples, and men used them in sacred rituals. Later, they were used during festivals to decorate gates and windows. After hundreds of years' development, now they have become a very popular means of decoration among country folk, especially women.

T: How delicate! Then how can they be made?

G: The main cutting tools are simple: paper and scissors or an engraving knife. It is easy to learn about cutting a piece of paper but very difficult to master it with perfection. One must grasp the knife in an upright fashion and press evenly on the paper with some strength. Flexibility is required but any hesitation or wiggling will lead to imprecision or damage the whole image. People find hope and comfort in expressing wishes with paper cuttings.

T: What does this big red paper character mean?

G: This is called "Xi". It means happiness. It's a traditional must on the newlywed's door. Upon the birthday party of a senior, the character "Shou" represents longevity and will add delight to the whole celebration; while this one, a pattern of plump children cuddling fish signifies that every year they will be abundant in wealth.

T: Oh, they're so rich in content. I will be this lovely rabbit.

G: It will bring good luck to you. Let's have a look at these kites. In ancient China the kite was known as "Zhiyuan" (paper glede). It has a history of more than 2000 years. Uses of kite have been changed several times in history. According to historical record, kite was first used in military. In the mid Tang Dynasty (618-907), in which the society was stable and peaceful, the use of kites was gradually changed from military to entertainment. With the innovation of papermaking, the raw material of kite changed from silk to paper. Kite became popular among civilians with a richer variety of forms. Kite-flying is now believed to be good for the health.

T: Miss Chen, what are these bottles called?

G: They are cloisonné, also Jingtailan. This is a unique art form that originated in Beijing during the Yuan Dynasty. The art of Jingtailan is a unique combination of sculpture, painting, porcelain making and copper-smithing. All the products are beautiful and elegant in molding, brilliant and dazzling in colors and splendid and graceful in design. It is a

Unit 7 China's Local Specialties

famous local handicraft in Beijing region. Jingtailan can be found on large objects such as vases and other large utensils and decorative items, as well as small items like earrings, bracelets, chopsticks or jars.

T: I see. Thank you very much for your introduction.

Knowledge Improvement

Traditional Chinese decorative knots, also known as Chinese knots, are typical local arts of China. They are a distinctive and traditional Chinese folk handicraft woven separately from one piece of thread and named according to its shape and meaning. In Chinese, "knot" means reunion, friendliness, peace, warmth, marriage, love, etc. Chinese knots are often used to express good wishes, including happiness, prosperity, love and the absence of evil. The endless variations and elegant patterns of the Chinese knot, as well as the multitude of different materials that can be used (cotton, flax, silk, nylon, leather and precious metals, such as gold and silver, to name a few) have expanded the functions and widened the applications of the Chinese knot. Jewelry, clothes, gift-wrapping and furniture can be accentuated with unique Chinese knot creations. Large Chinese knot wall hangings have the same decorative value as fine paintings or photographs, and are perfectly suitable for decorating a parlor or study. The Chinese knot, with its classic elegance and ever-changing variations, is both practical and ornamental, fully reflecting the grace and depth of Chinese culture.

Activity 1: Group discussion.

All the students in the classroom are divided into several groups to discuss what important information about the handicrafts are mentioned in the dialogue, after discussion, each group choose a representative to make a presentation, and then the teacher should give the comment on students' answer.

Activity 2: Make up a dialogue.

Please practice the dialogue for 5 minutes with your deskmates. After that, the teacher names some students to choose a role to make up a dialogue and then gives comments on their performance if necessary.

Activity 3: Simulated guiding.

All the students in the classroom are divided into several groups, and every group member may try to act as a local guide in class to simulate a situation of introducing a famous handiwork. Some phrases and expressions you have learnt may be used in your commentary.

Part C   Reading

Words List

brocade	/brəˈkeid/	n.	锦缎
embroidery	/imˈbrɔidəri/	n.	刺绣品；刺绣
manufacture	/ˌmænjuˈfæktʃə(r)/	v.	生产
silkworm	/ˈsilkwəːm/	n.	蚕
exquisite	/ikˈskwizit/	adj.	精美的；精致的
sophisticated	/səˈfistikeitid/	adj.	复杂巧妙的；水平高的
damask	/ˈdæməsk/	n.	花缎；锦缎
gauze	/gɔːz/	n.	薄纱
waterproof	/ˈwɔːtəpruːf/	adj.	不透水的；防水的
exalted	/igˈzɔːltid/	adj.	地位高的；兴奋的
flossy	/ˈflɔsi/	adj.	华丽的
epitomize	/iˈpitəmaiz/	v.	成为……的典范
crafsmanship	/ˈkrɑːftsmənʃip/	n.	精工细作
tribute	/ˈtribjuːt/	n.	贡品；贡献
connotation	/ˌkɔnəˈteiʃn/	n.	含义；隐含意义
gorgeous	/ˈgɔːdʒəs/	adj.	非常漂亮的；华丽的
unrestrained	/ˌʌnriˈstreind/	adj.	不受限制的；放纵的
manual	/ˈmænjuəl/	adj.	手工的；用手的
satin	/ˈsætin/	n.	缎子
aristocrat	/ˈæristəkræt/	n.	贵族
entail	/inˈteil/	v.	使必要；需要
filature	/ˈfilətʃə/	n.	缫丝
warp	/wɔːp/	n.	经线；经纱
shuttle	/ˈʃʌtl/	n.	梭子
intersperse	/ˌintəˈspəːs/	v.	散布；散置；点缀
multilayered	/ˈmʌltileiəd/	adj.	多层性
embrace	/imˈbreis/	v.	包括；包含
geometric	/ˌdʒiːəˈmetrik/	adj.	几何（学）的
scepter	/ˈseptə(r)/	n.	节杖，权杖
vulgar	/ˈvʌlgə(r)/	adj.	庸俗的；粗野的
luxuriant	/lʌgˈʒuəriənt/	adj.	华丽的；富饶的
primitive	/ˈprimətiv/	adj.	原始的
propitious	/prəˈpiʃəs/	adj.	吉庆的，吉祥的
tartan	/ˈtɑːtn/	n.	花格图案
lotus	/ˈləutəs/	n.	莲花图案

Unit 7 China's Local Specialties

tortoiseshell	/ˈtɔːtəʃel/	n.	蛱蝶
diversified	/daiˈvəːsifaid/	adj.	多变化的；各种的
immortality	/ˌiməˈtæləti/	n.	永生；不朽；不灭
phoenix	/ˈfiːniks/	n.	凤凰；长生鸟
auspicious	/ɔːˈspiʃəs/	adj.	吉利的；吉祥的
regenerate	/riˈdʒenəreit/	v.	使振兴；再生
unearth	/ʌnˈəːθ/	v.	发现；发掘
demonstrate	/ˈdemənstreit/	v.	表达；表露
surpass	/səˈpɑːs/	v.	超过；胜过
incorporate	/inˈkɔːpəreit/	v.	将……包括在内
prosperous	/ˈprɔspərəs/	adj.	繁荣的；成功的
promote	/prəˈməut/	v.	促进；推动
incite	/inˈsait/	v.	引起；鼓动

Useful Expressions

in terms of	在……方面
be characterized by	特点是……
be imbued with	充满
be in decline	衰微
experienced one's heyday	处于全盛时期
enter a new phase	步入新阶段
textile manufacturing	纺织品生产
mulberry tree	桑树
Oriental gem	东方明珠

Proper Nouns

Yun Brocade	云锦
Song Brocade	宋锦
Shu Brocade	蜀锦
Zhijin	织锦
Kujin	库锦
Kuduan	库缎
Zhuanghua	妆花
Dahualou Wooden Loom	大花楼木织机
Silk City	丝绸之都
Big Brocade	大锦
Box Brocade	合锦
Small Brocade	小锦
Su embroidery	苏绣
Xiang embroidery	湘绣

Yue embroidery	粤绣
Shu embroidery	蜀绣
No 1 Tomb of Mawangdui	马王堆 1 号墓
Fahua Buddhist Scripture	法华佛经
Panama Expo	巴拿马博览会

Chinese Brocade and Embroidery

China is a country with a rich heritage of textile manufacturing. Ancient Chinese textiles developed to an advanced stage in terms of growing cotton, flax, and mulberry trees, as well as keeping silkworms, using minerals and plants as dyes, and developing textile equipment. Of all the different Chinese textiles, silk is the most popular one all over the world, and the exquisite appearance of silk made silk manufacturing an important and sophisticated handcraft industry in ancient China.

China silk fabric styles consist mainly of open-work silk, brocade, damask, thin silk, gauze, and thick waterproof silk. Among all ancient fabrics, silk cloth known as jin represents the top of the industry's arts and crafts. The Chinese styles, Yun Brocade of Nanjing, Song Brocade of Suzhou and Shu Brocade of Sichuan enjoy an exalted reputation both at home and abroad.

Yun Brocade

Nanjing Yunjin, with a history of more than 1500 years, refers to the incredibly beautiful brocade made in Nanjing, capital city of eastern Jiangsu province. Yun in Chinese means "clouds", and jin means "brocade". The image is lovely: A delicate and flossy piece of brocade that feels just like soft clouds and is more valuable than gold. An inch of Nanjing brocade was said to be as valuable as an ounce of gold.

Nanjing Yunjin epitomizes the brocade craftsmanship over the past years. Ranking first among three major kinds of brocade in ancient China, it was a royal tribute respectively in the Yuan, Ming and Qing Dynasties. Due to its rich connotation of culture, science and technology, it is regarded by experts as the last milestone in the history of brocade craftsmanship in ancient China, publicly acknowledged as an "Oriental gem "and a "Wonder of China". It is also one of the most precious historic and cultural heritages of the Chinese nation and the world.

Nanjing Yunjin features rich patterns, big flowers, beautiful shapes, gorgeous and unrestrained colors, particularly the application of gold and peacock feather threads, free color-matching and changeable tints.

The varieties of Nanjing Yunjin are composed of "Zhijin", "Kujin", "Kuduan" and "Zhuanghua". The techniques of "swivel coiled weaving" and "varying color from flower to flower" in Zhuanghua cannot be handled by modern machines even nowadays. An inch of Yunjin is said to be as valuable as an ounce of gold. It is woven by a Dahualou Wooden

Unit 7 China's Local Specialties

Loom, 5.6 meters long, 1.4 meters wide and 4 meters high, through coordinated manual operation of a Zhuanghua worker and a weaver.

Song Brocade

Song Brocade, as its name implies, is a kind of brocade developed during the Song Dynasty (960-1279). It is mainly produced in Suzhou, the ancient "Silk City". and hence is also called Suzhou Song Brocade. As an ancient city of silk famous in China, Suzhou has been recognized as the land of brocade and satin. It is characterized by its bright color, exquisite patterns, and solid but soft texture.

The history of Suzhou Song Brocade can be traced back to the Spring and Autumn Period (770-476 B.C.). At that time, a large amount of brocade was already used by aristocrats from the Kingdom of Wu, which was located to the south of the Yangtze River.

The production of traditional Song Brocade entails numerous procedures. Usually there are over twenty procedures involved in producing it, from filature and dyeing to its completion. Not only are patterns woven in a structure of warps interspersed with wefts, but multicolored shuttles are cast in different combinations as well, in order to change the colors of the pattern. Such unique techniques give birth to brocade with multilayered and multicolored threads.

In terms of the artistic style, Song Brocade embraces variable geometric figures as its overall framework. Inside the framework, there are patterns involving flowers, ornamental scepters and clouds (the latter two indicate good fortune). Moreover, different colors that jointly characterize a piece of brocade coexist in harmony and contrast. In this way, brocade is beautiful yet not vulgar, simple yet elegant.

Song Brocade can be categorized according to the structure, craftsmanship, quality of the materials, thickness of brocade and the utility. Generally there are three categories of Song Brocade, namely, Big Brocade, Box Brocade, and Small Brocade.

Shu Brocade

Shu Brocade is one of the most important cultural heritages and well-known traditional craftworks of China.

Shu Brocade, with a history of about more than two thousand years, spent its silver in Qing and Han Dynasties, and had its golden time in Tang and Song Dynasties. Shu Brocade is featured for luxuriant appearance, bright color, primitive and elegant pattern, meaningful and propitious design, and imbued with rich folkloric and regional characteristic. The Shu Brocade in Tang Dynasty had various patterns such as tartan, lotus, tortoiseshell pattern, beads, and beasts. In late Tang Dynasty, the patterns became even diversified. The motifs on weft-patterned Shu Brocade include lanterns, balls, lion, lark, crane, peacock, and different kinds of followers. The traditional patterns are crane and plant of immortality, phoenix worshiped by a hundred birds, a bumper grain harvest, magpie and plum blossom, and phoenix and peony, which all have auspicious and fortunate meanings. It is really bright pearl in the weaving of brocade of our country.

Embroidery is a traditional Chinese craft which consists of pulling colored threads through a background material with embroidery needles to stitch colored patterns that have been previously designed on the ground. The adoption of different needling methods resulted in different embroidery styles and technique schools. Chinese embroidery had already reached a high level early in the Qin and Han Dynasties, and silk and embroidery were the main products transported along the ancient Chinese Silk Road. The four famous Chinese embroidery styles are the Su embroidery of Jiangsu province, the Xiang embroidery of Hunan province, the Yue embroidery of Guangdong province and the Shu embroidery of Sichuan province.

Su Embroidery

With a history of more than 3000 years, Su embroidery is the general name for embroidery products in areas around Suzhou, Jiangsu province. The craft, which dates back to the Three Kingdoms Period (220-280), became a sideline of people in the Suzhou area during the Ming Dynasty (1368-1644). Well known for its smoothness and delicateness, Su embroidery won Suzhou the title City of Embroidery in the Qing Dynasty. In the mid and late Qing, Su embroidery experienced further developments involving works of double-sided embroidering. There were 65 embroidery stores in Suzhou City. During the Republic of China period (1912-1949), the Su embroidery industry was in decline due to frequent wars and it was restored and regenerated after the founding of new China. In 1950, the central government set up research centers for Su embroidery and launched training courses for the study of embroidery. Weaving methods have climbed from 18 to the present 40.

Su embroidery features a strong, folk flavor and its weaving techniques are characterized by the following: the product surface must be flat, the rim must be neat, the needle must be thin, the lines must be dense, the color must be harmonious and bright and the picture must be even. Su embroidery products fall into three major categories: costumes, decorations for halls and crafts for daily use, which integrate decorative and practical values. Double-sided embroidery is an excellent representative of Su embroidery.

Xiang Embroidery

Xiang embroidery is well known for its time-honored history, excellent craftsmanship and unique style. The earliest piece of Xiang embroidery was unearthed at the No 1 Tomb of Mawangdui, Changsha City of the Han Dynasty (206 B.C.-A.D. 220). The weaving technique was almost the same as the one used in modern times, which demonstrated that embroidery had already existed in the Han Dynasty. In its later development, Xiang embroidery absorbed the characteristics of traditional Chinese paintings and formed its own unique characteristics. Xiang embroidery experienced its heyday at the end of the Qing Dynasty (1644-1911) and in the early Republic of China (early 20th century), even surpassing Su embroidery. After the founding of the People's Republic of China, Xiang embroidery was further improved and developed to a new level.

Xiang embroidery uses pure silk, hard satin, soft satin and nylon as its material, which is connected with colorful silk threads. Absorbing the spirit of Chinese paintings, the embroidery reaches a high artistic level. Xiang embroidery crafts include valuable works of art, as well as materials for daily use.

Shu Embroidery

Also called Chuan embroidery, Shu embroidery is the general name for embroidery products in areas around Chengdu, Sichuan province. Shu embroidery enjoys a long history. As early as the Han Dynasty, Shu embroidery was already famous. The central government even designated an office in this area for its administration. During the Five Dynasties and Ten States periods (907-960), a peaceful society and large demand provided advanced conditions for the rapid development of the Shu embroidery industry. Shu embroidery experienced its peak development in the Song Dynasty (960-1279), ranking first in both production and excellence. In the mid-Qing Dynasty, the Shu embroidery industry was formed. After the founding of the People's Republic of China, Shu embroidery factories were set up and the craft entered a new phase of development, using innovative techniques and a larger variety of forms.

Originating among the folk people in the west of Sichuan province, Shu embroidery formed its own unique characteristics: smooth, bright, neat and influenced by the geographical environment, customs and cultures. The works incorporated flowers, leaves, animals, mountains, rivers and human figures as their themes. Altogether, there are 122 approaches in 12 categories for weaving. The craftsmanship of Shu embroidery involves a combination of fine arts, aesthetics and practical uses, such as the facings of quits, pillowcases, coats, shoots and screen covers.

Yue Embroidery

Also called Guang embroidery, Yue embroidery is a general name for embroidery products of the regions of Guangzhou, Shantou, Zhongshan, Fanyu and Shunde in Guangdong province. According to historical records, in the first year of Yongyuan's reign (805) during the Tang Dynasty (618-907), a girl named Lu Meiniang embroidered the seventh volume of the Fahua Buddhist Scripture on a piece of thin silk 30 cm long. And so, Yue embroidery became famous around the country. The prosperous Guangzhou Port of the Song Dynasty promoted the development of Yue embroidery, which began to be exported at that time. During the Qing Dynasty, people used animal hair as the raw material for Yue embroidery, which made the works more vivid. During Qianlong's reign (1736-1796) of the Qing, an industrial organization was established in Guangzhou. At that time, a large number of craftsmen devoted themselves to the craft, inciting further improvements to the weaving technique. Since 1915, the work of Yue embroidery garnered several awards at the Panama Expo.

Influenced by national folk art, Yue embroidery formed its own unique characteristics. The embroidered pictures are mainly of dragons and phoenixes, and flowers and birds, with neat designs and strong, contrasting colors. Floss, thread and gold-and-silk thread embroidery are used to produce costumes, decorations for halls and crafts for daily use.

Activity 1: Choose the correct answer to complete the following sentences.

1. Which brocade features rich patterns, big flowers, beautiful shapes, gorgeous and unrestrained colors?
    A. Yunjin   B. Songjin   C. Shujin
2. Which city is called the "silk city"?
    A. Nanjing   B. Suzhou   C. Hangzhou
3. Which embroidery does double-sided embroidery represent for?
    A. Su embroidery   B. Xiang embroidery   C. Yue embroidery
4. When did Shu embroidery experience its peak development?
    A. in the Tang Dynasty   B. in the Song Dynasty   C. in the Ming Dynasty
5. How many approaches are there for weaving Shu embroidery?
    A. 120   B. 12   C. 122

Activity 2: Fill in the table according to what you have learnt.

Brocade	Place for Origin	Time for Origin	Features
Yun Brocade			
Song Brocade			
Shu Brocade			

Activity 3: Answer the following open questions in brief.

1. Why was Yunjin acknowledged as an "Oriental gem" and a "Wonder of China"?
2. Can you tell the history of Xiang embroidery?
3. What are the main features of Shu embroidery?
4. Which style of embroidery do you like? Why?
5. How to protect the traditional handicrafts, like brocade and embroidery?

Part D   Writing

Reschedule an Itinerary

在旅游行程中，当发生不可抗力危及旅游者人身和财产安全，或者非旅行社责任造成的意外情形，旅行社不得不调整或者变更旅游合同约定的行程安排时，全陪应报告组团社，由组团社作出决定并通知有关地方接待社，导游人员要将变更的行程及时通知给旅游者。变更行程时，有时需要延长，有时需要缩短，有时需要代替其中的某些内容。导游要根据实际情况进行迅速、及时、合情合理的处理。

Unit 7 China's Local Specialties

Sample

根据以下提示重新制订一份行程。

成都永胜旅行社计划接待山东济南某旅行团，一行 38 人将于 2010 年 7 月 27 日抵达成都，并计划在成都、九寨沟、黄龙、茂县 4 个地方共停留 6 天 5 晚。旅游活动进行第三天的时候，由于天气骤变，第四天去黄龙的行程改为去游牟尼沟风景区——扎噶瀑布，第五天下午九寨天气转晴，第六天的自由活动取消，最后及时送午餐，品尝成都小吃，游客登机离境。

Date	Route	Accommodation	Meals
7/27	Flight from J'inan to Chengdu and get settled in hotel	Chengdu	×××
7/28	Chengdu—Jiuzhaigou AM: Fuhe valley, Tibetan and Qiang Minority flirtatious expressions, Pingwu Bao'ensi PM: Dujuan Mountain	Jiuzhai	Breakfast Lunch Dinner
7/29	Jiuzhaigou National Park	Jiuzhai	Breakfast × Dinner
7/30	Jiuzhaigou—Munigou Jiutang Drug Store, Anduo local specialties store, Jiuhuangdijia crystal shop, Munigou	Jiuzhai or Chuanzhusi	Breakfast Lunch Dinner
7/31	Huanglong—Jiuzhai—Chengdu Tibetan horn comb shop	Chengdu	BreakfastLunch ×
8/1	urban park, Tea House, watch Chuan Opera, tast snacks, hot pot		Breakfast ××

Simulated Writing

Directions: Please use the words, phrases or expressions you have learnt to reschedule an itinerary according to the Chinese tips.

北京海洋旅行社计划接待山东济南某旅行团，一行 23 人将于 2010 年 8 月 27 日抵达北京，并计划在北京停留 4 天 3 晚。旅游活动进行第三天的时候，由于早上天气骤变，准备去八达岭长城的行程改为先去游景泰蓝工艺基地，第三天下午北京天气转晴，第四天去景泰蓝的时间改为去八达岭长城，最后坐火车离境。

Part E   Practical Training

Training item 1: Oral Presentation

Directions: You are required to work with your group members to finish the task in this part. Every group should choose a kind of Chinese ancient vessels you are familiar to give an introduction. After preparation and practice, a group member will be asked to make an oral presentation; other students may have additional remarks or explanation if necessary. And then teacher gives comments on students' performance.

Training item 2: Role-play

Directions: All the students in the class are divided into several groups, every member in the group choose one role to perform. Students should use the language they have learnt as far as possible.

Situation 1: Ms. Brown, a tourist from USA, comes to Shaanxi province. A local guide Lily is showing her around Shu Yuan Men (The Arts Street)—a well-known street in the style of ancient towns in Xi'an. Lily is introducing the knowledge of Chinese handicrafts like the shadow puppets, paper cuts, kites, etc..

Situation 2: Ms. Brown is very interested in China Yun Brocade, and a local guide Lily is giving her brief introduction of China brocade. In addition, Lily offers her more knowledge about other famous brocade like Song Brocade and Shu Brocade.

Situation 3: Lily, a local guide from China Yunnan International Travel Service. She is providing service for the tourists who are travelling in Yunnan province. They have to change their original plan for the third day because of the sudden rainfall. Now she is rescheduling the itinerary and telling the result to the tourists.

Training item 3: Outside-class Work

Directions: Please find some information about other famous handicrafts in China from books, Internet or some other channels. Try to compare and explain some characteristics of them and then make a brief introduction.

Knowledge links

China's Three Porcelain Capitals

Jingdezhen in Jiangxi Province

Since the period of *Han Dynasty* (hàn dài 汉代), Jingdezhen has had the ceramic industry. Up to now, it has more than 2000 years of history. Jingdezhen's porcelain has been famous not only in China but also in the world. It became known internationally for being "as thin as paper, as white as jade, as bright as a mirror, and as sound as a bell". *Qinghua*

Unit 7　China's Local Specialties

Porcelain (qīng huā 青花), *Linglong Porcelain* (líng lóng 玲珑), *Fencai Porcelain* (fěn cǎi 粉彩) and *Seyou Porcelain* (sè yòu 色釉) altogether are called Four Traditionally Famous Porcelains in Jingdezhen.

Dehua in Fujian Province

Liling in Hunan Province

Five kinds of Chinese Tea

Green Tea

Green Tea is the most natural of all Chinese tea classes. It's picked, natural dried, and then fried briefly (a process called "killing the green") to get rid of its grassy smell. Fermentation process is skipped.

Green Tea has the most medical value and the least caffeine content of all Chinese tea classes. Aroma is medium to high, flavor is light to medium.

About 50% of China's teas are Green Tea. The famous Green Tea in China is in Sichuan, Zhejiang provinces.

Black Tea

Chinese Black Tea produces a full-bodies amber when brewed. Black Tea undergoes withering (drying), left to ferment for a long while, and then roasted. Black Tea leaves become completely oxidized after processing.

Black Tea has a robust taste with a mild aroma. It contains the highest amount of caffeine in Chinese tea classes.

Red Tea

Red leaves and red tea color, it's characteristic of Red Tea's fermentation process.

There are 3 subclasses of Chinese Red Tea – "Kung Fu Red Tea", "Ted Tea Bits" and "Small Species Red Tea".

Chinese Red Tea has low aroma and medium flavor

Flower/Scented Tea

Chinese Flower Tea is an unique class of Chinese tea. It subdivides into Flower Tea and Scented Tea.

Flower Tea is a simple concept that dried flowers are used, without much processing, to make tea. Scented Tea uses green tea, red tea as base and mixes with scent of flowers.

Chinese Flower Tea has light to medium flavor and medium to strong aroma.

Sichuan and Yunnan province are the best place to buy flower tea, for example jasmine flower tea and green tea is the specialty of Sichuan and there is a tea mountain called Mengding Shan.

Oolong Tea

Oolong Tea is Japanese favorite and said to lose weight. It is half way between green tea and black tea in a sense that it's half-fermented. It's also called "Qing Cha" (grass tea).

Typical Oolong Tea leaves are green in the middle and red on the edges as a result of the process to soften tea leaves.

Oolong Tea leaves are withered and spread before undergoing a brief fermentation process. Then Oolong Tea is fried, rolled and roasted.

Oolong tea is the chosen tea for the famous Kung Fu Cha brewing process. It's serious Chinese tea drinker's tea. Aroma ranges from light to medium. Beginners in Oolong Tea should be careful as even though flavor is only mild to medium, the tea could be strong.

Woodcut Chinese New Year Pictures

The woodcut New Year pictures are usually put up on windows or walls five days before the New Year's Day to express good wishes for the coming year.

Taohuawu Suzhou, Tianjin Yangliuqing, in Mianzhu, Sichuan and Shandong Weifang, China's famous woodcut New Year pictures of the four civil origin. New Year pictures in Mianzhu, Sichuan, Jiangsu Taohuawu, Tianjin Yangliuqing, Shandong Weifang Yang and Development of the board pictures in history has long enjoyed a good reputation, known as China's "Four pictures."

Tourism Resources in China

Unit 8

Topic Guidance

There are three types of tourism resources in China: natural sites, historical and cultural sites and folk customs.

China is rich in tourism resources.

China encompasses a great diversity of landscapes and a corresponding variety of natural resources and climate types.

Warming-up

Read the following questions and discuss with your partner.

1. Which scenic spot do you want to visit most in China? Why?
2. Where is your favorite resort for summer and winter holiday? Why?
3. Do you know the world heritage list of China? Can you list some?

Look at the following pictures and try to describe it in your own words.

Part A Listening

Words List

meandering	[miˈændəriŋ]	adj.	曲折的；蜿蜒的
grassland	/ˈɡrɑːslænd/	n.	草原；草地
relic	[ˈrelik]	n.	遗物；遗迹
folk	/fəʊk/	adj.	民俗的；传统民间的
category	/ˈkætəɡəri/	n.	种类；类别
biological	/ˌbaiəˈlɔdʒikl/	adj.	生物学的；生物的
meteorological	[ˌmiːtiərəˈlɔdʒikl]	adj.	气象的；气象学的
ancient	/ˈeinʃənt/	adj.	古代的；古老的
ruin	/ˈruːin/	n.	残垣断壁；废墟
irreplaceable	/ˌiriˈpleisəbl/	adj.	不可替代的；绝无仅有的
maintenance	/ˈmentənəns/	n.	维护；保养
landscape	/ˈlændskeip/	n.	风景；景色
decade	/ˈdekeid/	n.	十年；十年期

Useful Expressions

refer to	指的是
rich in	富有
tourism resources	旅游资源
tourism industry	旅游业
cultural relics	文化遗址
place of historical interest	名胜古迹
cultural remains	文化遗迹
under key protection	重点保护

Activity 1: Spot dictation.

Tourism resources are widely (1)_____ the things and factors in (2)_____, which attract tourists and create social, (3)_____, and which can be developed and used by (4)_____.

China is (5)_____ tourism resources. With green mountains, (6)_____, forests and (7)_____, it has attracted visitors all over the world. With thousands years of history, China has a great number of (8)_____ and (9)_____ across the country.

Tourism resources in China can be (10)_____ into three groups: (11)_____, historical and cultural sites, and (12)_____. They can be further divided into eight categories: land scenery, waters scenery, (13)_____ scenery, meteorological scenery,

Unit 8 Tourism Resources in China

(14)_____, architecture and facilities, (15)_____, and people's activities.

The (16)_____ sources are shared by people in the world. In order to protect them, the Chinese government has devoted great efforts to the protection, (17)_____ of natural landscapes and cultural remains. Over the past 5decades since the founding of (18) _____, governments and tourist organizations have made great contributions. At home the Chinese government has listed (19)_____ as "famous Chinese historical and cultural cities" (20)_____ up to now.

Activity 2: Decide whether the following statements are True or False while listening to the paragraph again.

(   ) 1. Tourism resources can create economic benefits only.

(   ) 2. Plants and animals are also considered as part of the tourism resources in China.

(   ) 3. Folk customs is not considered to be part of tourism resources in China.

(   ) 4. Great efforts have been done to protect tourism resources in the past two decades.

(   ) 5. 110 cities have been listed as "famous Chinese historical cities" without any protection.

Activity 3: Choose the correct answer while you are listening.

1. How many kinds of national park are mentioned in the conversation?
    A. 5   B. 7   C. 9

2. Which of the following scenic spots is listed as one of the Eight Wonders in the world?
    A. The Temple of Heaven.
    B. The Summer Palace.
    C. The Great Wall.

3. Why did the emperors go to climb Mount Taishan after taking the throne?
    A. To enjoy the beautiful scenery there.
    B. To show their great power.
    C. To worship their ancestors.

4. Where is the largest grassland best reserved in China?
    A. Qinghai
    B. Hulunbeier
    C. Xinjiang

5. Which is the longest river in China? And how long is it?
    A. The Yangtze River, 6211 kilometers.
    B. The Amazon, 6400 kilometers.
    C. The Nile, 6650 kilometers.

Part B Speaking

Words List

identify	/aɪˈdentɪfaɪ/	v.	确认；视为
geographic	/ˌdʒiəˈɡræfɪk/	adv.	地理学的；地理的
unique	/juˈnik/	adj.	唯一的；独一无二的
reputation	/ˌrepjuˈteɪʃn/	n.	名誉；名声
divine	/dɪˈvaɪn/	adj.	天赐的；神授的
sacrifice	/ˈsækrəˈfaɪs/	n.	祭祀；祭献
inspiration	/ˌɪnspəˈreɪʃn/	n.	灵感；启发
belittled	/bɪˈlɪtld/	adj.	渺小的；微不足道的
undoubtedly	/ʌnˈdaʊtɪdli/	adv.	毫无疑问地；肯定地
heritage	/ˈherɪtɪdʒ/	n.	遗产；继承物

Useful Expressions

be considered as	被认为
pray to	祈祷
in regard to	就……而言
thermal resource	热资源
UNESCO	联合国教科文组织

Proper Nouns

Dongyi culture	东夷文化
Da Wenkou culture	大汶口文化
Longshan culture	龙山文化
the Early Morning Sunrise to the East	旭日东升
the Glowing Sunset in the West	晚霞夕照
the Sea of Clouds	云海玉盘
the Golden Belt along the Yellow River	黄河金带
Eighteen Paths	十八盘
Heavenly Queen Pool	王母池
Mid-heaven Gate	中天门
Dongyue Temple	岱庙
Black Dragon Pool	黑龙池

Unit 8　Tourism Resources in China

Situational dialogue

Miss Li Hua, a local guide from China Shandong International Travel Service, is showing guests from America around a famous mountain—Mount Taishan, the leader of the "Five Scared Mountains" in China.

T: tourists　　G: local guide

G: Good morning, ladies and gentlemen, now we are driving towards Mt. Taishan. We'll be at the foot of it half an hour later. When we mention mountains in China, there's much to say. Mt. Taishan is located 43 miles to the south of Jinan, in the center of Shandong province. It is the first of the "Five Sacred Mountains" in China.

T: Miss Li, can you tell us what the "Five Sacred Mountains" are?

G: Yes. There are five famous mountains in China. According to the geographic locations, they are Mount Taishan to the east in Shandong province, Mount Huashan to the west in Shaanxi, Mount Hengshan to the north in Shanxi province, Mount Hengshan to the south in Hunan province, and Mount Songshan in the center in Henan province.

T: Then why Mount Taishan is the first of the five famous mountains?

G: Well, Mount Taishan is located in the middle of Shandong province, east of North China Plain. Since ancient times, it was thought to be the nearest mountain to the sun, and because it is one of the oldest mountains in the world, the mountain has gained great reputation over thousands of years. In ancient China, emperors used to visit Mount Taishan to pray to the heaven, earth and their ancestors, as it is believed that the mountain is a holy mountain and divine mountain. According to historical records, there were 72 emperors making sacrifices to Mount Taishan in the past dynasties. And now Mount Taishan is considered as a symbol of Chinese people and Chinese nation. Meanwhile, the mountain has given inspiration to a lot of poets and literary scholars. It is so great and splendid that there is a famous saying, that "When one climbs up on Mount Taishan, the world below him seems to be suddenly belittled".

T: Oh, that sounds interesting.

G: Yes. Mount Taishan is rich in natural resources, such as water and thermal energy. Mount Taishan was a developed area in the ancient times. It was the center of Dongyi Culture in regard to its historical position. Being in the center of Qi and Lu, there was Da Wenkou Culture in the south foot and Longshan Culture in its north foot. The mountain is located in the key position where the railway from the central plains of China to Shandong Peninsula meets the railway connecting the south and north part of China in the east coast. All these conditions help Mount Taishan to be the first among the "Five Sacred Mountains" in China.

T: Miss Li, can you introduce us the most famous sceneries of the mountain?

G: Sure. The four greatest wonders of the mountain are: the Early Morning Sunrise to the East, the Glowing Sunset in the West, the Sea of Clouds and the Golden Belt along the Yellow River. Besides, there are also attractive scenic spots, such as Eighteen Paths,

Heavenly Queen Pool, Mid-heaven Gate, Dongyue Temple, Black Dragon Pool, and so on. In 1987, Mount Taishan was listed in the UNESCO's World Natural and Cultural Heritage List. Those beautiful sceneries will undoubtedly encourage visitors to visit this place and make them reluctant to leave.

T: This mountain is really amazing. After listening to your introduction, I am looking forward to paying a close look at it. So wonderful! Thanks for your good introduction.

G: You are welcome. OK, we are arriving. Please take your bags, and let's get off the bus. Follow me, please.

Knowledge Improvement

China is well-known for many other famous mountains, such as the four sacred peaks of Buddhism, Mount Huangshan, Mount Lushan, and so on. Mountain areas cover two-thirds of our country.

Buddhism claims the most followers of any religion in China, and there are four mountains worshipped by the faithful: Mount Wutai in Shanxi, Mount Emei in Sichuan, Mount Jiuhua in Anhui and Mount Putuo in Zhejiang.

Mount Huangshan in Southern Anhui is well known for its karst formations clouds pine trees and hot springs. It is shrouded in seas of clouds about 200 days a year. And it becomes one of the main attractions in the area. Pine trees grow on precipices, with strange shapes as they cling to the rocks. The "Yingke Pine Tree" is a local landmark to show warm welcome to visitors. The mountain is very popular with traditional Chinese landscape painters, because of its unique attractions and sceneries.

Mount Lushan is located in northern Jiangxi province. Like Mount Huangshan, it is also famous for seas of clouds and mists, which become especially active during the summer solstice. In winter the clouds drop down to earth, and the mountain tries in vain to peak through the formations. Mount Lushan is also well known for its summer resort facilities.

Activity 1: Group discussion.

All the students in the classroom are divided into several groups to discuss what important information about the Mount Taishan are mentioned in the dialogue, after discussion, each group choose a representative to make a presentation, and then the teacher should gives the comments on the students' answer.

Activity 2: Make up a dialogue.

Please practice the dialogue for 5 minutes with your desk mates. After that, the teacher names some students to choose a role to make up a dialogue and then give comments on their performance if necessary.

Unit 8 Tourism Resources in China

Activity 3: Simulated guiding.

All the students in the classroom are divided into several groups, and every group member may try to act as a local guide in class to simulate a situation of introducing a famous mountain. Some phrases and expressions you have learnt may be used in your commentary.

Part C   Reading

Words List

civilization	/ˌsivəlaiˈzeiʃn/	n.	文明；文化
ethnic	/ˈeθnik/	adj.	民族的；种族的
minority	/maiˈnɔrəti/	n.	少数人；少数民族
convention	/kənˈvenʃn/	n.	公约；协定
cave	/keiv/	n.	山洞；洞穴
waterfall	/ˈwɔːtəfɔːl/	n.	瀑布；巨瀑
autonomous	/ɔːˈtɔnəməs/	adj.	自主的；自治的
crystal	/ˈkristl/	adj.	清澈透明的；晶莹的
renowned	/riˈnaund/	adj.	著名的；闻名的
shoal	/ʃəul/	n.	浅滩；暗滩
reef	/riːf/	n.	暗礁；礁石
lush	/lʌʃ/	adj.	繁茂的；茂盛的
greenery	/ˈɡriːnəri/	n.	草木；绿色植物
fairyland	/ˈfeərilænd/	n.	仙境；梦境
karst	/kɑːst/	n.	卡斯特地形
grotto	/ˈɡrɔtəu/	n.	石窟
cliff	/klif/	n.	悬崖；峭壁
sculpture	/ˈskʌlptʃə(r)/	n.	雕像；雕塑
superb	/suːˈpəːb/	adj.	极佳的；卓越的
craftsmen	/ˈkrɑːftsmən/	n.	工匠；工艺师
crisscross	/ˈkrisˌkrɔs/	v.	互相交叉
Neolithic	/ˌniːˈliθik/	adj.	新石器时代的
memorial	/məˈmɔːriəl/	adj.	纪念的；悼念的
arch	/ɑːtʃ/	n.	拱门；拱
civilian	/səˈviliən/	n.	平民；老百姓
diverse	/daiˈvəːs/	adj.	不同的；多样的
commemorate	/kəˈmeməreit/	v.	纪念
commercial	/kəˈməːʃl/	adj.	贸易的；商业的
matriarchal	/ˌmeitriˈɑːkl/	adj.	母系的；母权的
undulating	/ˈʌndjuleitiŋ/	adj.	起伏的；波动的

Useful Expressions

accede to	加入
apply for	申请
date back	追溯
hydro-power project	水利工程

Proper Nouns

the Three Gorges	三峡
The Lesser Three Gorges	小三峡
Silk Road	丝绸之路
Shaolin Temple	少林寺
Pingyao Ancient City	平遥古城
Shoton (Yogurt) Festival	雪顿节
Norbulingka	罗布林卡
Dalai Lamas	达赖喇嘛
Nadam Fair	那达慕大会
March Street	三月街

Tourism Resources in China

With a history of more than 7000 years, China has a great number of cultural relics and places of historical interests spread across the country. With a vast area of land, it is full of natural resources. Meanwhile, as a big family of 56 ethnic groups, Chinese culture and customs ethnic minorities are treasure stores of tourism resources.

China acceded to the Convention Concerning the Protection of the Cultural and Natural Heritage on December 12, 1985. The Chinese government has made constant efforts in applying for world heritage to the UNESCO since 1986. So far, 40 scenic resorts have been listed as the world cultural and/or natural heritage by the United Nations Educational, Scientific and Cultural Organization (UNESCO).

Tourism resources in China can be divided into three groups: natural sites, historical and cultural sites, and folk customs.

Natural Sites—China's lakes, valleys, caves and waterfalls

There are many spectacular lakes on the plateau in northern China. The Tianchi (Heavenly Pool) in the Tianshan Mountains in Xinjiang Autonomous Region is 1980 meters above sea level. This 105-meter-deep lake is crystal clear, surrounded by high mountains with green grass and colorful flowers.

There are many scenic spots and historical sites along the renowned Three Gorges of the Yangtze River. The Qutang Gorge is rugged and majestic. The Wuxia Gorge is elegant and deep. The Xiling Gorge is full of shoals, reefs, as well as rolling water. The Lesser

Unit 8 Tourism Resources in China

Three Gorges are lush with greenery, and the water is so clear that you can easily see to the bottom. The Three Gorges Dam built here is China's biggest key hydro-power project, contributing to one of China's greatest scenic spots.

Jiuzhaigou, Huangguoshu Waterfalls, and Guilin are all located in southwestern China. Jiuzhaigou is a beautiful "fairyland valley" in northern Sichuan province, running over 40 km through snow-covered mountains, lakes, waterfalls and forest. As a group of waterfalls, the Huangguoshu Waterfalls in Guizhou province, are famous for their splendid sceneries. With eighteen above-ground and four below, the waterfalls can be heard from 5 km away. The Lijiang River in Guangxi Zhuang Autonomous Region winding its way through karst peaks for 82 km between Guilin and Yangshuo, attracts tourists all over the world each year.

Historical and Cultural Sites

China is one of the earliest civilized regions in the world, and its long history has left many precious historical and cultural relics.

As a symbol of the Chinese nation, the Great Wall is a prime example of China's historical sites which have become one of the major tourist attractions in the country. The Chinese started to build the wall in 221 B.C. It is of huge bricks and stones. As the greatest defense-structure project in the history of human civilization, its history can be dated back to the Spring and Autumn period and the Warring States period, and it was used to protect the country from being invaded. It took two millennia to complete the construction. This magnificent project is one of the wonders in the history of human civilization. It is preserved as a historical site today, and 10 sections of the Great Wall are opened to tourists, including the passes, blockhouses and beacon towers at Badaling in Beijing, Laolongtou and Jiayuguan Pass.

Grottoes, cliff paintings and sculpture are also precious treasures of China's tourism resources. China's grottoes are mostly located along the ancient Silk Road. The best known are the Mogao Grottoes, Yungang Grottoes and Longmen Grottoes. Dunhuang Mogao Grottoes is also known as "Thousand Buddha Grottoes". According to historical records, the Grottoes were carved in 366 A.D., with 492 grottoes in existence covering about 45000 square meters of murals, and 415 painted clay figures, all of high creativity, artistry and imagination. The diversified grottoes are full of great Buddhism, art and social value that have attracted numerous visitors from all walks of life.

As the birthplace of Chinese Zen Buddhism, the Shaolin Temple is located in Mountain Song in Henan province. It was built in 495 during the Northern Wei Dynasty. It is also famous for its Shaolin Martial Arts. In Hubei province, the beautiful Wudang Mountain is also known for the martial arts and Taiji. The mountain is about 321 square kilometers in area. It attracts ever-growing numbers of tourists with its splendid natural sceneries, such as its 72 grotesque peak, springs, caves, streams and cliffs. As a sacred site of Taoism, the mountain preserves China's most complete, largest-scale and best ancient Taoist architecture.

There are 110 famous historical and cultural cities in China, most of which are over 1000 years old. To the south of the Yangtze River, Suzhou and Hangzhou, known as "paradise on earth" are crisscrossed with rivers, lakes, bridges, fields and villages, as beautiful as paintings. The well preserved Pingyao Ancient City, in central Shanxi province, 90 km southwest of the city of Taiyuan, was built in the Ming Dynasty. It is a site of Neolithic era Yangshao and Longshan cultures of 5000—6000 years ago. The ancient city of Lijiang lies at the northwest part of Yunnan Province and is the center of Naxi minority Dongba culture. The ancient culture of Naxi has a history of near 1000 years. The old city continues to maintain the original flavor of the local lifestyle, the typical groups of buildings and the profound cultural heritage of the region. As it was built in the Song Dynasty, the city has plenty of stone bridges, memorial arches and civilian houses. As a "living museum of ancient civilian houses", it provides us with precious materials for the study of the history of Chinese domestic architecture.

Folk Customs and Habits

The diverse cultures and life styles of China's 56 ethnic groups are reflected in their festivals and folk customs. There is a famous summer festival on the Mongolian grasslands, called the Nadam Fair. It has many attractions, including wrestling, horse racing and archery contests.

The Bai ethnic group is famous for the "March Street" festival which is celebrated on Diancang Mountain of Dali, Yunnan province. The festival is said to be associated with the Buddhist Goddess of Mercy who helps the Bai people by suppressing a devil. It has become a tradition to burn incense and make sacrifices to commemorate her virtues. Till now, the festival has become an annual gathering for people to take part in commercial, cultural and sports activities.

In Xishuangbanna, the Water-Sprinkling Festival of the Dai ethnic group is a lively springtime celebration. People take part in the dragon boat racing and peacock dances, and chase and pour water over each other as a symbol of good luck and happiness.

Mosuo people live around Lugu Lake in Southwest China, 2700 meters above the sea level. The ethnic group is famous for their matriarchal society, which empowers the women to be the chief of their groups, and be entitled to choose their husbands. It has a very special system of marriage, and is called the last women's kingdom on earth. The place is so mysterious that it has attracted a great number of tourists.

Activity 1: Choose the correct answer to complete the following sentences.

1. Tourism resources can be divided into _____ types in China.

    A. 3   B. 4   C. 5

2. When did China accede to the Convention Concerning the Protection of the Cultural and Natural Heritage?

    A. Since 1986   B. On December 12, 1985   C. By the end of 2001

Unit 8 Tourism Resources in China

3. The splendid Three Gorges are composed of Qutang Gorge, Wu Gorge and _____.
   A. Tiger-jumping Gorge   B. Kongling Gorge   C. Xiling Gorge

4. China's most complete, largest-scale and best ancient Taoist architecture is preserved in _____.
   A. Mount Emei   B. Mount Wudang   C. Mount Huangshan

5. The "March Street" is celebrated by _____ people.
   A. Bai   B. Dai   C. Mosuo

Activity 2: Fill in the blanks according to what you have learnt.

1. Jiuzhaigou in northern Sichuan province is a beautiful "_____" running over 40 km. The Huangguoshu Waterfalls are _____. The Lijiang River _____ through karst peaks for 82 km between Guilin and Yangshuo.

2. The history of the Great Wall can be dated back to _____ and _____ periods.

3. The best known Mogao Caves is a "_____" with 492 caves with murals and statues on the cliff face. The total area of the murals is _____ and there are over _____ colorful statues.

4. The ancient city of Lijiang in Yunnan province is the center of _____.

5. The Mosuo people live around Lugu Lake, _____ above the sea level is noted for _____ and is called _____.

Activity 3: Answer the following open questions in brief.

1. Can you name three famous mountains in China? Interpret one of them to a group of foreigners.

2. Can you introduce one of the famous waterfalls in China?

3. How much do you know about the four greatest grottoes in China?

4. Have you ever heard of Yin Xu? Can you say something about it?

5. How much do you know about the ancient sites and ruins in China?

Part D Writing

Compose an Accident Report

事故报告是导游员在带团中遇到问题、投诉或事故时撰写的书面材料。在撰写事故报告时，需要把事件发生的过程和处理结果简要叙述一遍，并要从中汲取经验教训，防微杜渐。事故报告力求准确、清楚、实事求是。

一般事故报告中需包含以下要点。

(1) 事故发生的时间、地点。(time and location)

(2) 受害人。(affected parties or individuals)

(3) 事故发生的经过。(description of the accident)

135

(4) 事故发生后所采取的补救及保护措施。(actions taken to solve the problem)

(5) 事故处理的结果。(solution)

Sample

Situation: A tour group from Canada arrives at Beijing to pay a visit to the Great Wall at 10 a.m., October 1st. Miss Li Hua, local guide from China Beijing International Travel Service, meets them and will be with them for the tour. During their visit to Badaling, Mary, one of the tourists gets lost and can't find the way back to the tour group, as she is deeply absorbed by the splendid scenery on the wall. Miss Li finds the problem immediately and calls the police station to help. With the help of the policeman, she finds Mary half an hour later.

Accident Report

Date of the incident: October 1st, 2010

Time of the incident: 10 a.m.

From: Li Hua

Description: On October 1st, 2010, I went to pick up a group of tourists from Canada and took them to the Great Wall. When we got to Badaling, I made an introduction to the scenery there and then gave the tourists some time to take pictures. As it was very crowded there, one of our tourists, Mary, got lost when we started to get to the next spot. When I noted that, I immediately called the nearby police station. With the help of three policemen, we finally found Mary half an hour later. She said that she was absorbed by the beautiful scenery on the Great Wall and totally forgot the time we arranged to get together. I sincerely apologized to Mary.

I learnt a lesson from this incident. Tour guide should be very careful in their work. More actions should be taken to avoid the missing of the guests.

Simulated Writing

Directions: Please use the words, phrases or expressions you have learnt to write a welcome speech according to the following instructions.

2011年2月10日14：00左右，旅行团来到天安门广场，一番游览过后，导游员李华安排了一个小时的自由活动。旅行团成员布朗先生在拍照时不小心站在了长安街的自行车道上。此时王先生正骑车由东向西行驶，由于车速较快，他看到布朗先生时，没有能够及时刹车，撞到了布朗先生。随后，在安排好团队其他成员后，李华随王先生陪同布朗先生前往就近的医院进行检查。经过医生的仔细检查，布朗先生并无大碍，王先生支付了检查费用并道歉。

虽然这起事故没有造成严重后果，但导游员应汲取经验教训，在日后工作中应避免类似事故的发生。

Unit 8 Tourism Resources in China

Part E   Practical Training

Training item 1: Oral Presentation

Directions: You are required to work with your group members to finish the task in this part. Every group should choose a kind of tourist resources you are familiar to give an introduction. After preparation and practice, a group member will be asked to make an oral presentation; other students may have additional remarks or explanation if necessary. And then the teacher gives comments on the students' performance.

Training item 2: Role-play

Directions: All the students in the class are divided into several groups, every member in the group choose one role to perform. Students should use the language they have learnt as far as possible.

Situation 1: Mr. Brown, a tourist from USA, comes to Shandong province. A local guide Lily is showing him around Mount Taishan——a very famous Mountain in China. Lily is introducing the knowledge of different kinds of mountains and their locations to Mr. Brown.

Situation 2: Mr. Brown is very interested in different tourism resources in China, and a local guide Lily is giving him brief introduction including natural sites, historical and cultural sites, and folk customs and habits. In addition, Lily shows him lots of typical example of those tourism resources.

Situation 3: Lily, a local guide from China Shandong International Travel Service, meets some problems and emergencies. She is now composing an accident report.

Training item 3: Outside-class Work

Directions: Please find some information about natural or human tourism resources in China from books, Internet or some other channels. Try to make a brief introduction.

Knowledge links

Major Tourism Resorts in China

Province	Major Tourism Resort
Anhui Province	Mount Huangshan, Chao Lake Scenic Spot, Mount Jiuhua
Beijing	Badaling Great Wall, the Forbidden City, the Summer Palace, the Runis of Yuanmingyuan Palace, the Temple of Heaven
Chongqing	Dazu Rock Carvings, Qutang Gorge, Wansheng Stone Forest, Wu Gorge, Xiling Gorge

续表

Province	Major Tourism Resort
Fujian Province	Gulangyu Island, Mount Gu Scenic Spot, Lin Zexu Memorial Hall, Mount Wuyi Scenic Spot
Gansu Province	Mount Maiji, Mirage, Mogao Grottoes
Guangdong Province	Mount Baiyun Scenic Spot, Huanghuagang Cemetery of Seventy-two Martyrs, Seven Star Rock, World Window
Guangxi Zhuang Autonomous Region	Liangfeng River National Forest Park, Li River, Elephant Trunk Hill, Xu Beihong' Former Residence
Guizhou Province	Chishui Scenic Spot, Huangguoshu Waterfall Scenic Spot, Sites of Zunyi Conference, Nine Dragon Cave Scenic Spot
Hainan Province	Ends of the Earth, Five-finger Mountain, Holiday Beach, Yalong Bay
Hebei Province	Baiyangdian Lake, Bashang Grassland, Chengde Mountain Resort, Mulan Hunting Ground, Shanhai Pass, Yansai Lake
Heilongjiang Province	Jingpo Lake Scenic Spot, St. Sophia Church, Sun Island, Wudalianchi Scenic Spot, Yabuli Skiing Resort
Henan Province	Mount Baiyun, Longmen Grottoes, Shaolin Temple, Mount Songshan, Mount Yuntai Scenic Zone
Hong Kong	Hong Kong Convention and Exhibition Center, Ocean Park, Qingma Bridge, Victoria Park
Hubei Province	Gezhou Dam, Huanghe Tower, Shennongjia, Mount Wudang,
Hunan Province	Dongting Lake, Mount Hengshan, Mount Shaoshan, Zhangjiajie National Forest Park
Inner Mongolia Autonomous Region	Daqing Gully Nature Reserve, Genghis Khan's Mausoleum, Grand Mosque, Zhaojun's Tomb
Jiangxi Province	Poyang Lake, Mount Jinggangshan, Jingdezhen Porcelain Museum,
Jiangsu Province	Ancient Canal, Huqiu Hillock, Qinhuai River, Tai Lake Scenic Spot, Dr, Sun Yet-san's Mausoleum
Jilin Province	Changbai Mountain, Changchun Film Studio and Film City, Songhua Lake Scenic Spot
Liaoning Province	Imperial Palace in Shenyang, Tiger Beach Park, Yalu River Scenic Spot
Macao	Big Barbette, Dasanba Memorial Arch, Mage Temple
Ningxia Hui Autonomous Region	Cliff Carvings of Helan Mountain, Imperial Mausoleums of the Western Xia Dynasty, Sand Lake
Qinghai Province	Mengdalin Nature Reserve, Qinghai Lake, Ta'er Monastery
Shaanxi Province	Mount Huashan Scenic Spot, Hukou Waterfall, Mount Tiantai, Zhao Mausoleum
Shandong Province	Baotu Spring, Cemetery of Confucius, Kong Family Mansion, Confucius's Temple, Mount Taishan, Mount Laoshan, Long Island, Penglai Pavilion

Unit 8 Tourism Resources in China

续表

Shanghai	Chenghuang Temple, Jinmao Edifice, Oriental Pearl Tower, The Band, Yuyan Garden,
Shanxi Province	Hukou Waterfall of the Yellow River, Longshan Grottoes, Pingyao Ancient City, Mount Wutai, Yungang Grottoes
Sichuan Province	Mount Emei, Jiuzhaigou Valleyt Scenic Spot, Leshan Big Buddha, Huanglong Scenic Spot, Dujiangyan Irrigation System
Taiwan Province	Danshui Scenic Spot, Sun and Moon Pools, Yangming Mountain
Tianjin	Dagukou Emplacement, Huangya Pass Great Wall, Yuhuang Pavilion
Tibet Autonomous Region	Everest, Jokhang Temple, Norbu Lingka, Potala Palace
Xinjiang Uygur Autonomous Region	Bostan Lake, Flame Mountain, Karez Well, Loulan Ancient City, Tianchi Lake of Tianshan Mountain
Yunnan Province	Dianchi Lake, Erhai Lake, Lijiang Ancient City, Stone Forest Scenic Spot, Jade Dragon Jokul
Zhejiang Province	Mount Putuo Scenic Spot, Qiandao Lake, Mount Tianmu, West Lake Scenic Spot, Mount Yandang

Overview of Chinese Tourist Zone Distribution

Unit 9

Topic Guidance

China has a long history of over 5000 years.

The vast areas of the land and long coastline have blessed the country with magnificent and colorful landscapes.

China attracts more and more visitors to come and explore its beauty and mystery.

Warming-up

Read the following questions and discuss with your partner.
1. How much do you know about Chinese Tourist Zone?
2. Have you ever read anything about the Forbidden City?
3. Do you know any of Chinese ancient cities?

Look at the following pictures and try to describe it in your own words.

Unit 9 Overview of Chinese Tourist Zone Distribution

Part A Listening

Words List

spectacular	/spek'tækjələ(r)/	adj.	壮观的；壮丽的
ethnic	/'eθnik/	adj.	民族的；种族的；部落的
delicacy	/'delikəsi/	n.	1. 柔软(性)；脆弱；娇嫩 2. 精美的食物；佳肴
attract	/ə'trækt/	v.	吸引；使喜爱；引起……的好感
bless	/bles/	v.	求上帝降福；祝福
gorgeous	/'gɔːdʒəs/	adj.	非常漂亮的；美丽动人的
canyon	/'kænjən/	n.	(周围有悬崖峭壁的)峡谷
steep	/stiːp/	adj.	陡的；陡峭的
desolate	/'desələt/	adj.	无人居住的；荒无人烟的
crystal	/'kristl/	n.	结晶；晶体
appreciate	/ə'priːʃieit/	v.	欣赏；赏识；重视
majestic	/mə'dʒestik/	adj.	雄伟的；威严的；壮观的
elegant	/'eligənt/	adj.	文雅的；优美的；漂亮的
industrious	/in'dʌstriəs/	adj.	勤奋的；勤劳的；忙碌的
circulation	/ˌsɜːkjə'leiʃn/	n.	传递；流传；流通
allusion	/ə'luːʒn/	n.	间接提到；典故
glorious	/'glɔːriəs/	adj.	值得称道的；光荣的；荣耀的
comparatively	/kəm'pærətivli/	adv.	比较上；相对地
potential	/pə'tenʃl/	adj.	潜在的；可能的
mystery	/'mistri/	n.	神秘的事物；不可理解之事

Useful Expressions

due to	因为；由于
as well as	和……一样；和；也
accompanied by	伴随着
at present	目前；现在
thanks to	幸亏；由于

Proper Nouns

Terra Cotta Warriors	兵马俑
Forbidden City	紫禁城，中国明清两代 24 个皇帝的皇宫。明朝第

三位皇帝朱棣在夺取帝位后，决定迁都北京，即开始营造紫禁城宫殿，至明永乐十八年(1420 年)落成。依照中国古代星象学说，紫微垣(即北极星)位于中天，乃天帝所居，天人对应，是以皇帝的居所又称紫禁城。

Activity 1: Spot dictation.

China is rich in tourist attractions. The nature has endowed it with spectacular views. Over 5000 year's long history has (1)_____ . The 56 ethnic groups make the country's folk customs so colorful. (2)_____, plus unique music, drama and world-known delicacy, China attracts large crowds of tourists from home and abroad every year. The vast areas of the land and long coastline have (3)_____ magnificent and colorful landscapes. Here, you can see gorgeous canyons, as well as steep mountains; evergreen tropical rain forest, (4)_____ ; desolate deserts, as well as crystal lakes. The major natural landscape types in the world can be found in this beautiful land. To appreciate the wild beauty, you can go to Qinghai-Tibet Plateau (5)_____ . To appreciate the majestic beauty, go to Himalaya Mountains, which will tell you (6)_____ . To appreciate the elegant beauty, please visit the (7)_____ in southern China. And also the industrious Chinese ancient laboring people had created innumerable world wonders such as the Great Wall, the Terra Cotta Warriors and the Forbidden City, accompanied by the circulation of many stories and allusions. China has over 100 historical and cultural cities, many of which have a history of over 1000 years. Strolling in these cities, you will feel (8)_____ and this is perhaps the best way to understand (9)_____. At present, China has formed a tourism market with a comparatively large scale, (10)_____. China, thanks to its unique charm, attracts more and more visitors to come and explore its beauty and mystery.

Activity 2: Decide whether the following statements are True or False while listening to the paragraph again.

(   ) 1. China is rich in tourist attractions.

(   ) 2. To appreciate the wild beauty, you can go to Himalaya Mountains.

(   ) 3. Winding rivers and tender water towns are mostly seen in southern China.

(   ) 4. China has over 100 historical and cultural cities, many of which have a history of over 100 years.

(   ) 5. China, thanks to its fast growth, attracts more and more visitors to come.

Unit 9 Overview of Chinese Tourist Zone Distribution

Activity 3: Choose the correct answer while you are listening.

1. In which year the Great Wall of China was listed as a World Heritage by UNESCO?
   A. 1987　　　　　　　B. 1988　　　　　　　C. 1985
2. Where is the hometown of Confucius?
   A. Qi　　　　　　　　B. Qufu　　　　　　　C. Kongfu
3. How many of these gardens are still in a good state of preservation?
   A. 9　　　　　　　　B. 10　　　　　　　　C. 11
4. How high is Potala Palace?
   A. 3767.1　　　　　　B. 3767.17　　　　　　C. 3767.19
5. When will the Museum of Terracotta Civil Officials be closed?
   A. 6:00p.m.　　　　　B. 6:30p.m.　　　　　　C.7:00p.m.

Part B　Speaking

Words List

relic	/ˈrelik/	n.	遗风；遗俗
heritage	/ˈheritidʒ/	n.	遗产
combination	/ˌkɔmbiˈneiʃn/	n.	结合体；联合体；混合体
resource	/riˈsɔːs/	n.	资源；财力；才智；谋略
landscape	/ˈlændskeip/	n.	风景；景色
splendid	/ˈsplendid/	adj.	壮丽的；雄伟的
classify	/ˈklæsifai/	v.	划分；区分
enthusiasm	/inˈθjuːziæzəm/	n.	热情；热心
grotto	/ˈgrɔtəu/	n.	人工洞室；石窟
gem	/dʒem/	n.	宝石
mansion	/ˈmænʃn/	n.	公馆；宅第
cemetery	/ˈsemətri/	n.	墓地；坟地；公墓
participate	/pɑːˈtisipeit/	v.	参加；参与
splash	/splæʃ/	v.	泼洒
oyster	/ˈɔistə(r)/	n.	牡蛎；蚝

Useful Expressions

be divided into	被分成；被分为
hundreds of	数以百计的；成百上千
an old China hand	中国通

143

be classified into	把……分为
The world would be her oyster	人生最得意的时刻
participate in	参加；参与

Proper Nouns

Water - Splashing Festival	泼水节是傣族最隆重的节日，也是云南少数民族中影响面最大、参加人数最多的节日。泼水节是傣族的新年，相当于公历的四月中旬，一般持续 3 至 7 天。第一天傣语叫"麦日"，与农历的除夕相似；第二天傣语叫"恼日"(空日)；第三天是新年，叫"叭网玛"，意为岁首，人们把这一天视为最美好、最吉祥的日子。
Nadan Fair	那达慕大会，那达慕是中国蒙古族人民具有鲜明民族特色的传统活动，也是蒙古族人民喜爱的一种传统体育活动形式。"那达慕"是蒙古语的译音，意为"娱乐、游戏"，以表示丰收的喜悦之情。每年农历六月初四(多在草绿花红、羊肥马壮的阳历七八月)开始的那达慕，是草原上一年一度的传统盛会。
tug-of-war	拔河

Situational dialogue

Miss Li Hua, a local guide from China International Travel Service, is giving suggestion to Johnson, her guest from Canada on Chinese tourist zones.

J: Johnson　　　L: Li Hua

J: Li, I've heard too much of China. My friends, who have been to China, also always tell me no matter what you are interested in, whether it is cultural relics, natural heritages or the combinations of both, in China you will unexpectedly find pleasant surprise. Could you give me some advice if I want to travel in China?

L: Yes, you are welcome. Generally speaking, China's tourist resources can be primarily divided into three parts: natural landscape, manmade attractions and folk customs. Which part are you most interested in?

J: How about starting from manmade attractions? I know China has hundreds of famous mountains and waters, and I know the long Chinese history and splendid culture have left countless sites of historic interest.

L: Well, Johnson, you really show your enthusiasm for China!

Unit 9 Overview of Chinese Tourist Zone Distribution

J: I told you! And friends call me an old China hand even though I still have a long way to go.

L: (With a smile) The historic relics in China can be classified into three groups: holy place of religious culture, rock paintings and grottos, and famous historical and cultural cities. To see the holy place of religious culture, you will get to know how the three main world's religion as well as Chinese native Taoism developed in the country. The rock paintings and grottos are the gem and the symbol of Chinese ancient art treasure.

J: Yeah, I know that. I know the Forbidden City and the Summer Palace in Beijing, Terracotta Warriors in Xi'an, Mogao Caves in Dunhuang, Confucius Temple and Cemetery of Confucius, and the Kong Family Mansion in Qufu, Classical Gardens of Suzhou…What are folk customs, anyway?

L: You must know China is a big family of 56 ethnic groups.

J: I know, and my girlfriend likes the ethnic costume very much.

L: Well, each of these ethnics differs in traditional culture and life styles. For example, Dai People, mainly living in Xishuangbanna of Yunnan province, hold Water-Splashing Festival each year. On this day, people will chase and splash water on each other as they think water is the symbol of luck and happiness. Nadam Fair is Mongolian's annual pageant which is held between July and August. On this important festival, sport activities such as horseracing, wrestling, tug-of-war and ball games are held, attracting many local people to take part in and visitors to watch. Participate in these colorful activities, and you will learn more about the country's diversified culture.

J: I can't wait to go. By the way, where should I go, as my girlfriend wants to buy back some gifts?

L: If your girlfriend wants to go shopping, the best choice is Hong Kong. People always say: giving a person a blank check and telling her to go shopping in Hong Kong is like putting a kid in a candy store. The world would be her oyster. Hong Kong has everything one could ever dream of.

J: Thanks a million, Li. You really do me a great favor.

Knowledge Improvement

How many cultural experiences have you lived? Have you ever go around China to enjoy its wonders? No matter what you are interested in, whether it is cultural relics, natural heritages or the combinations of both, in China you will unexpectedly find pleasant surprise.

The following table is the list of cultural and natural heritage of China.

Name	Year of Recognition	Category	Location
the Great Wall of China	1987	Cultural Heritage	Beijing
Mogao Grottoes	1987	Cultural Heritage	Dunhuang
Imperial Palaces of the Ming and Qing Dynasties: the Forbidden City, Shenyang Imperial Palace	1987	Cultural Heritage	Beijing and Shenyang
Mausoleum of the First Qin Emperor Palace	1987	Cultural Heritage	Xi'an
Peking Man Site at Zhoukoudian	1987	Cultural Heritage	Beijing
Mount Taishan	1987	Cultural and Natural Heritage	Shandong
Mount Huangshan (The Yellow Mountains)	1990	Cultural and Natural Heritage	Huangshan
Jiuzhaigou Valley Scenic and Historic Interest Area	1992	Natural Heritage	Sichuan
Mount Emei Scenic Spot and Leshan Giant Buddha Scenic Spot	1992	Cultural and Natural Heritage	Sichuan
Huanglong Scenic and historic Interest Area	1992	Natural Heritage	Sichuan
Wulingyuan Scenic and Historic Interest Area	1992	Natural Heritage	Zhangjiajie
Potala Palace	1994	Cultural Heritage	Lhasa
Chengde Summer Palace	1994	Cultural Heritage	Chengde
Ancient Building Complex in the Wudang Mountains	1994	Cultural Heritage	Hubei
Temple and Cemetery of Confucius and the Kong Family Mansion	1994	Cultural Heritage	Shandong
Lushan National Park	1996	Cultural Heritage	Jiangxi
Suzhou Gardens: Lion Grove, Humble Administrator Garden, Lingering Garden, Garden of Master of the Nets	1997	Cultural Heritage	Suzhou
Pingyao Ancient Town	1997	Cultural Heritage	Pingyao
Old Town Lijiang	1997	Cultural Heritage	Lijiang
the Summer Palace	1998	Cultural Heritage	Beijing
the Temple of Heaven	1998	Cultural Heritage	Beijing

Unit 9 Overview of Chinese Tourist Zone Distribution

续表

Name	Year of Recognition	Category	Location
Dazu Rock Carvings	1999	Cultural Heritage	Chongqing
Mount Wuyi	1999	Cultural Heritage	Xiamen
Xidi Village and Hongcun Village	2000	Cultural Heritage	Huangshan
Imperial Tombs of the Ming and Qing Dynasties	2000	Cultural Heritage	Beijing
Longmen Grottoes	2000	Cultural Heritage	Luoyang
Qingchengshan Mountain and Dujiangyan Irrigation Project	2000	Cultural Heritage	Sichuan
Yungang Grottoes	2001	Cultural Heritage	Datong
Three Parallel Rivers of Yunnan Protected Areas	2003	Natural Heritage	Yunnan
Capital Cities and Tombs of the Ancient Koguryo Kingdom	2004	Cultural Heritage	Jilin
Historic Centre of Macau	2005	Cultural Heritage	Macau
Sichuan Giant Panda Sanctuaries: Wolong, Mt Siguniang and Jiajin Mountains	2006	Natural Heritage	Sichuan
Yin Xu	2006	Cultural Heritage	Anyang
South China Karst	2007	Natural Heritage	South China
Kaiping Diaolou and Villages	2007	Cultural Heritage	Guangdong
Fujian Tulou	2008	Cultural Heritage	Fujian
Mount Sanqingshan National Park	2008	Natural Heritage	Jiangxi
Wutai Mountain	2009	Cultural Heritage	Shanxi
Shaolin Temple	2010	Cultural Heritage	Zhengzhou
Danxia Landform	2010	Natural Heritage	South China

Activity 1: Group discussion.

All the students in the classroom are divided into several groups to discuss how many places are mentioned in the dialogue and what do you know about them, after discussion, each group choose a representative to make a presentation, and then the teacher should gives the comments on the students' answer.

Activity 2: Make up a dialogue.

Please practice the dialogue for 5 minutes with your desk mates. After that, teacher names some students to choose a role to make up a dialogue and then give comments on their performance if necessary.

Activity 3: Simulated guiding.

All the students in the classroom are divided into several groups, and every group member may try to act as a tour guide in class to simulate a situation of describing a place listed in the part of *Knowledge improvement*. Some phrases and expressions you have learnt may be used in your commentary.

Part C   Reading

Words List

splendor	/ˈsplendə/	n.	壮观；辉煌；杰出
elevation	/ˌeliˈveiʃn/	n.	1. 高度；(尤指)海拔 2. 晋级；提升
contrast	/kənˈtrɑːst/	v.	对比；对照
offshore	/ˌɒfˈʃɔː(r)/	adj.	近海的；离岸的
peninsula	/pəˈninsjələ/	n.	半岛
remarkable	/riˈmɑːkəbl/	adj.	显著的；引人注目的
tremendous	/trəˈmendəs/	adj.	极大的；精彩的
rough	/rʌf/	adj.	不确切的；粗略的
estimate	/ˈestimeit/	v.	估价；估算
unique	/juˈniːk/	adj.	唯一的；独一无二的
magnificent	/mæɡˈnifisnt/	adj.	壮丽的；宏伟的；值得赞扬的
icon	/ˈaikɒn/	n.	图标；图符；偶像
representative	/ˌrepriˈzentətiv/	n.	代表；典型人物；代表性人物
revere	/riˈviə/	v.	尊敬；崇敬；敬畏
precipitous	/priˈsipitəs/	adj.	险峻的；峭拔的
epitomize	/iˈpitəmaiz/	v.	成为……的典范(或典型)
masculine	/ˈmæskjəlin/	adj.	男人的；像男人的；阳性的
grandeur	/ˈɡrændʒə(r)/	n.	宏伟；壮丽；堂皇
grotesque	/ɡrəʊˈtesk/	adj.	奇形怪状的；丑陋的；奇异的
yearn	/jɜːn/	v.	渴望；渴求
convey	/kənˈvei/	v.	表达；传递
equator	/iˈkweitə(r)/	n.	赤道
vital	/ˈvaitl/	adj.	必不可少的；对……极重要的
astonishing	/əˈstɒniʃiŋ/	adj.	难以置信的
fertilize	/ˈfɜːtəlaiz/	v.	施肥于
islet	/ˈailət/	n.	小岛
resplendent	/riˈsplendənt/	adj.	辉煌的；灿烂的；华丽的
brilliant	/ˈbriliənt/	adj.	聪颖的；技艺高的

Unit 9 Overview of Chinese Tourist Zone Distribution

excavation	/ˌekskəˈveiʃn/	n.	(对古物的)发掘；挖掘
prosperity	/prɔˈsperəti/	n.	兴旺；繁荣
engrave	/inˈgreiv/	v.	在……上雕刻
vigor	/ˈvigə/	n.	气势；力度；魄力
accumulation	/əˌkjuːmjuˈleiʃən/	n.	积累；积聚；堆积
oriental	/ˌɔːriˈentl/	adj.	东方(尤指中国和日本)的；东方人的

Useful Expressions

by contrast	比较起来；与之相反；与……形成对比的是
have a tremendous influence on	有着巨大的影响
give birth to	生下

Proper Nouns

Turfan	吐鲁番，又称"火州"，位于中国新疆天山东部山间盆地。
Lake Ayding	艾丁湖，中国最低的湖泊——月色美人艾丁湖。在吐鲁番盆地南部，是一个盐湖。湖面海拔-154m，是全国最低的洼地，也是世界上主要洼地之一。由于湖水不断蒸发，大部分湖面已变为深厚的盐层。艾丁湖又名觉洛浣，艾丁湖维吾尔语意为月光湖，以湖水似月光皎洁美丽而得名。
Potala Palace	布达拉宫俗称"第二普陀山"，屹立在西藏首府拉萨市区西北的红山上，是一座规模宏大的宫堡式建筑群。最初是松赞干布为迎娶文成公主而兴建的，17世纪重建后，布达拉宫成为历代达赖喇嘛的冬宫居所，也是西藏政教合一的统治中心。整座宫殿具有鲜明的藏式风格，依山而建，气势雄伟。布达拉宫中还收藏了无数的珍宝，堪称是一座艺术的殿堂。
Hakka	客家人；客家语

Travel in China

The topography of China is marked by many splendors. Mount Everest (Qomolangma Feng), situated on the border between China and Nepal, is the highest peak in the world, at an elevation of 29035 feet (8850m). By contrast, the lowest part of the Turfan Depression in the Uygur Autonomous Region of Xinjiang—Lake Ayding—is 508 feet (155m) below sea level. The coast of China contrasts greatly between south and north. To the south of the bay of Hangzhou, the coast is rocky and indented with many harbors and offshore islands. To the north, except along the Shandong and Liaodong peninsulas, the coast is sandy and flat.

Among them, the most remarkable feature of China's relief is the vast extent of its mountain chains; the mountains indeed have exerted a tremendous influence on the country's political, economic and cultural development. By rough estimate, about one-third of the total area of China consists of mountains.

A mountain has its unique character: magnificent, imposing or elegant. The Five Most Famous Mountains can be the representative of all mountains in China. Mount Taishan in Shandong is the most revered; Shaolin Temple brought worldwide fame to the Song Mountain in Henan; Mt Huashan in Shaanxi is precipitous; Hengshan in Shanxi has jagged ranges and Mt. Hengshan in Hunan is elegant in appearance.

Many mountains epitomize different religions and cultures. Mt. Jiuhua in Anhui, Mt. Emei in Sichuan, Mt. Putuoshan in Zhejiang and Mt. Wutai in Shanxi are the most noted Buddhist holy mountains. While Mt. Huangshan in Anhui, Mt. Laoshan in Shandong, Wudang Mountain in Hubei, Mount Wuyi in Fujian, Mt. Qingcheng in Sichuan and Dragon and Tiger Mountain in Jiangxi are well-known Taoist holy mountains. Mt. Huangshan seems to enjoy exceptionally high reputation. It is said to boast of combining the masculine grandeur of Mount Taishan, the mist and clouds of Hengshan in Hunan, and the grotesque splendor of Mt. Huashan. That's why the old saying goes as having no wish to see any of the five most famous mountains if having seen Mt. Huangshan.

In China, Mountains and waters often occur together in literary works to express great breadth of mind or yearning for nature. They usually hold more than what their facial beauty can convey.

If joined together, the natural rivers of China reach a total length 10.5 times greater than the length of the Earth's equator. Among all the rivers, the Yellow River is affectionately known as the mother river of Chinese nation. The Yangtze River, the world third longest, enjoys great fame because of the numerous historic relics found along its banks and the beautiful legends about this vital waterway. Holding enchanting riverside scenery, Li River gathers the most astonishing natural beauty of northeast Guangxi by connecting Guilin and Yangshuo.

Poyang, Dongting and Taihu Lakes are the top three freshwater lakes in China, which fertilize the fields around and make them towns of rice and fish. West Lake, the golden name card of Hangzhou and Thousand Islets Lake (Qian Dao Hu), the resplendent pearl of the city are hot scenic spots. Qinghai Lake, the largest inland salt lake in China, has the Bird Island as its most charming part, attracting lots of tourists.

In addition, Beidaihe Scenic Spot, Qingdao Seashore Scenic Area, Beihai Silver Beach and Asian Dragon Bay (Yalong Wan) have top beaches for summer holiday.

Vast field gives birth to many beautiful mountains and rivers. And Time-honored history and brilliant Chinese civilization endow the country with numerous historical and cultural relics.

Unit 9 Overview of Chinese Tourist Zone Distribution

Numerous historic relics from China's long history have been preserved. Among them, the Great Wall of China is the icon of the Chinese nation and the most popular attraction. The excavation of Yin Xu (Yin Ruins) in Anyang City of Henan Province let the world know Oracles which have been proved to be the earliest written character of human beings. Potala Palace in holy Lhasa is a splendid and complicated building complex on the Red Hill, being the political center of Tibet.

Another place gathering multitudes of historical and culture relics should be the Silk Road, a vital trading route that traversed Asia and Europe. The prosperity of the past has gone. But communications in commodity, religion and ideology between the west and the east have been vividly engraved in places along the road and continue to inspire vigor in new era.

Beijing and Xi'an will occur to one's mind at the mention of ancient cities with profound cultural accumulations. Undoubtedly, Museum of Terra Cotta Warriors can best represent the city which was the capital of the first feudal dynasty, Qin (221 B.C.-206 B.C.). While Beijing is most highlighted by the Forbidden City, the imperial palace of the Ming and Qing Dynasty which symbolized the peak hours of Chinese feudal society and where the imperial power completely faded out of the country.

Zhouzhuang in Suzhou is known as the number one water town in China. In the same city, Tongli is regarded as the oriental Venice. In Zhejiang province Wuzhen city, you will find waterside pavilions which are seldom seen in ancient water towns in southern China. Now the town is a fine base for movies and televisions.

Ancient City of Pingyao in Shanxi is characterized by the city wall and the ancient compounds of rich families. Xidi and Hongcun Ancient Villages have typical local residences in southern Anhui province. Lijiang Old Town and Dali Ancient City in Yunnan have delicate residential houses, lanes and streams. In addition, Beijing's courtyards, earth towers of the Hakkas in Fuzhou, Huizhou local residences in Anhui and the farmers' caves in Shaanxi are outstanding representatives of local residences in different areas of China.

Besides all of these, Scenic areas and natural reserves are built to better protect the intactness and original flavor of some sights from damage of tourists. Jiuzhaigou Valley and Huanglong scenic and historic interest area are the most popular destinations especially famous for the beauty of colorful lakes. Zhangjiajie and Wulingyuan scenic spots are wonderful options for walking among luxury forests. If you are interested in the culture and life styles of Chinese ethnic minorities, their villages and buildings best show you their distinctive flavors. China Folk Culture Villages in Guangdong and Nationality Culture Park in Yunnan are comprehensive scenic areas to gather flavors of many ethnic groups together in one place.

Activity 1: Choose the correct answer to complete the following sentences.

1. Where is the lowest place of China?
   A. Nepal   B. Turfan   C. Liaodong peninsula
2. Which mountain does it refer to in the old saying " having no wish to see any of the five most famous mountains if having seen it."
   A. Mt. Huangshan   B. Mt. Putuoshan   C. Mt. Qingcheng
3. _____ has the Bird Island as its most charming part.
   A. Dongting Lake   B. Taihu Lake   C. Qinghai Lake
4. In which city you can find the oriental Venice?
   A. Hangzhou   B. Wuzhen   C. Suzhou
5. Which of the following is not true?
   A. Beijing and Xi'an are ancient cities with profound cultural accumulations.
   B. Huanglong scenic and historic interest area are the most popular destinations for walking among luxury forests.
   C. You can see many ethnic groups together in Yunnan.

Activity 2: Fill in the blanks with the words given below. Change the form if necessary.

astonish   exert   contrast   engrave   estimate

1. He _____ the two different economic systems in his speech.
2. Even though the teacher told him not to be so selfish, he never _____ himself to help anyone.
3. The painter's _____ for painting the whole house was at least 1000 dollars.
4. I am just surfing on line. There is a (an) _____ news about Shaolin Temple.
5. The novel, as a love story, is to _____ the younger generation in the special times.

Activity 3: Answer the following open questions in brief.

1. What do you know about Mount Everest in addition to the information mentioned in the reading?
2. What do you know on Chinese mountain chains? Try to name at least 3 of them.
3. There are so many cities that have their special characters such as Zhouzhuang in Suzhou called water town, Pingyao in Shanxi called an ancient city, and what about your city? Try to describe it.
4. Do you know Chinese 7 famous ancient capital? Try to list them and their scenic spots.
5. How much do you know about Xishuangbanna?

Unit 9 Overview of Chinese Tourist Zone Distribution

Part D Writing

Compose a Farewell Speech

"欢送词"是导游接待工作的尾声,是对行程的小结。这时导游与游客已经熟悉甚至成为朋友。如果说"欢迎词"给游客留下美好和深刻的第一印象是重要的,那么,在送别时致好"欢送词",给游客留下的印象将会是持久和终生难忘的!"欢送词"除要有好的文采外,更要有感情包含其中。

规范的"欢送词"应包含5个要素:表示惜别、感谢合作、小结旅游、征求意见、期盼重逢。

表示惜别是指在欢送词中应含有对分别的惋惜留恋之情,讲此内容时不可嬉皮笑脸以免留下人走茶凉的印象。

感谢合作是指感谢游客在旅游中对导游工作的支持、合作、帮助和谅解。

小结旅游是指与游客一起回忆一下这段时间所游览的项目或参加的活动等,帮助游客加深印象,将感官的认识上升到理性的认识。

征求意见是询问游客在导游过程中我们还存在着哪些不足,希望大家批评指正,以便下次接待能让游客更加满意。

期盼重逢是要表达对游客的情谊,希望能再次为游客服务。

Sample

Situation: A tour group from Canada will go back home after their visit. Miss Li Xiaohua, a local guide from China International Travel Service, is delivering a farewell speech to the tourists on behalf of China International Travel Service.

Farewell Speech

Ladies and gentlemen,

Time flies so quickly and your visit to Shandong province is drawing to a close. Before your leaving, I would like to say a few words. First thanks everybody in the group for having been very co-operative, friendly, understanding and punctual. As your tour guide, I feel pretty appreciated.

I hope you enjoyed your visiting here, and I am sure next time you will be more enjoyable when you come again!

This is the beginning of our friendship; we believe it will last forever. I am looking forward to seeing you again in the near future. Thank you again for explaining in tourism of my support and help, and if there be any inadequacies, criticism please!

Welcome to Shandong province again.

Bye- bye!

Simulated Writing

Directions: Please use the words, phrases or expressions you have learnt to write a farewell speech according to the Chinese tips.

我们的旅程马上就要结束了，我也要跟大家说再见了，临别之际没什么送大家的，就送大家四个字吧。首先第一个字是缘，缘分的缘，俗话说"百年修得同船渡，千年修得共枕眠"，那么和大家5天的共处，算算也是千年的缘分了；接下来这个字也是原，原谅的原，在这几天中，有什么做的不好的地方，希望大家多多包涵，在这里说声对不起了；再一个字是圆满的圆，此次行程圆满结束多亏了大家对我工作的支持和配合，谢谢了；最后一个字还是源，财源的源，祝大家财源犹如滔滔江水连绵不绝，也祝大家身体好，工作好，今天好，明天好，现在好，将来好，好上加好！

Part E Practical Training

Training item 1: Oral Presentation

Directions: You are required to work with your group members to finish the task in this part. Every group should choose a tourist region you are familiar to give a description. After preparation and practice, a group member will be asked to make an oral presentation; other students may have additional remarks or explanation if necessary.

Training item 2: Role-play

Directions: All the students in the class are divided into several groups, every member in the group choose one role to perform. Students should use the language they have learnt as far as possible.

Situation 1: Ms. Brown, a tourist from USA, comes to your place. A local guide Lily is showing her around and introducing the knowledge and characteristics of a famous tourist region in China.

Situation 2: Lily, a local guide from China International Travel Service, is sending tourists from England to the airport. Now, she is delivering a farewell speech.

Training item 3: Outside-class Work

Directions: Please find some other information about Chinese tourist regions which you are interested in from books, Internet or some other channels. Try to compare and explain the characteristics of them and then make a brief introduction.

Knowledge links

Eight major tourist regions of China and its representatives

Tourist area in Northeast China

The Shenyang Imperial Palace

The Shenyang Imperial Palace, located at No. 171, Shenyang Road, Shenhe District in Shenyang City, is the only existing royal palace in China outside of the Forbidden City in

Unit 9 Overview of Chinese Tourist Zone Distribution

Beijing. The main structure of the palace was built in 1625 when Nurhachi was in power. It was finished in 1636 by his son Abahai (Huangtaiji). Nurhachi and Abahai were both founding emperors of the Qing Dynasty.

Covering an area of more than 60000 square meters (about 71760 square yards), the Shenyang Imperial Palace is one twelfth the size of the Forbidden City in Beijing. The palace consists of more than 300 rooms, formed around 20 courtyards. The Shenyang Imperial Palace houses have many ancient cultural relics, such as Nurhachi's sword and Abahai's broadsword. There are also many artworks displayed there, such as paintings, calligraphy, pottery, sculptures and lacquer ware.

The Changbai Mountains

The Changbai Shan or "Forever White Mountains", broken by occasional open valleys, reach elevations mostly between 450 and 900m. In some parts the scenery is characterized by rugged peaks and precipitous cliffs. The highest peak is the volcanic cone of Mount Baitou (2744m), which has a beautiful crater lake at its snow-covered summit. As one of the major forest areas of China, the region is the source of many valuable furs and famous medicinal herbs.

Tourist area in North China

Ming Tombs

50 km northwest from Beijing City lies the Ming Tombs—the general name given to the mausoleums(陵园) of 13 emperors of the Ming Dynasty (1368—1644). The mausoleums have been perfectly preserved, as has the necropolis of each of the many emperors. Because of its long history, palatial and integrated architecture, the site has a high cultural and historic value. The layout and arrangement of all thirteen mausoleums are very similar but vary in size as well as in the complexity of their structures. Changling, the chief of the Ming Tombs, is the largest in scale and is completely preserved. The total internal area of the main building is 1956 square meters. There are 32 huge posts, and the largest measures about 14 meters in height.

Tourist area in the middle and lower Yellow River

Qufu Confucius Temple (Kong Miao)

Located inside the south gate of Qufu, Shandong, the Temple of Confucius is a group of grand buildings built in oriental style. Together with the Summer Palace in Beijing and the Mountain Resort of Chengde, the Temple of Confucius in Qufu is one of the three largest ancient architectural complexes in China.

The Temple started as three houses in the year of 478 B.C., the second year after the death of Confucius. The existing Temple of Confucius was rebuilt and renovated during the Ming (1368—1644) and Qing (1644—1911) Dynasties. Patterned after a royal palace, it is divided into nine courtyards. Altogether there are 466 rooms and 54 gateways covering an area of 218000 square meters (2346609 square feet). The yellow tiles and red walls all covered with delicate decoration make the Temple extremely grand.

Tourist area in northwest

Pingyao County

With an area of 1260 square kilometers, it has 5 towns and 9 villages under its prefecture. Unlike those cities or counties in the south of the Yangtze River, Pingyao, simple and steeped in ancient tradition, was not endowed with charming natural scenery but with a group of accomplished businessmen. Pingyao was the birthplace of the Jin Businessmen, who were one of the two famous Chinese business groups during the Ming and Qing Dynasties. Owing to this, the first Chinese exchange shop was opened in Pingyao. Then, for the next hundred years, Pingyao was home to almost all of the large exchange shops in China. To a certain degree, Pingyao was to China during the eighteenth century what Wall Street is to the US, which not only helped promote the economic development of Shanxi, but also left us with a magnificent old city and a series of grand residences.

Tourist area in South China

Guilin

"East or west, Guilin landscape is best!" On account of the natural beauty and historic treasures, Guilin is considered to be the pearl of China's thriving tourist industry. The strangely shaped hills or karsts, with the verdant vegetation ranging from bamboos to conifers together with crystal clear waters and wonderful caves make Guilin such an appealing destination.

Tourist area in southwest

Jiuzhaigou Valley Scenic and Historic Interest Area

It is said that if there should be wonderlands on the earth, Jiuzhaigou Valley must be one of them. There is no equal elsewhere that has sceneries and fables of dreamlike eloquence, or natural purities like a fairyland as Jiuzhaigou Valley. It combines blue lakes, waterfalls, verdant forests, snow-covered mountains.

Tourist area in Tibet

Heavenly Lake Namtso (纳木错)

In Nov. 14, 2005, Namtso Lake in the Tibet Autonomous Region was selected as one of the five most beautiful lakes in China by Chinese National Geography magazine. Namtso Lake's touching beauty should not be missed by any traveler who visits Tibet. Its purity and solemnness are symbols of Qinghai-Tibet Plateau. In Tibetan, Namtso means "Heavenly Lake." It is considered one of the three holy lakes in Tibet. Namtso is famous for its high altitude (4720m), vast area (1961 square kilometers) and beautiful scenery.

Unit 9　Overview of Chinese Tourist Zone Distribution

Being the second largest saltwater lake in China only after Qinghai Lake, Namtso Lake is the biggest lake throughout Tibet and also the highest altitude saltwater lake in the world. The water here is a storybook crystal-clear blue. Clear skies join the surface of the lake in the distance, creating an integrated, scenic vista. Soul of every visitor who has ever been here seems to be cleansed by the pure lake water.

Tourist area in the middle and lower Yangtze

Yellow Mountain (Huangshan Mountain)

Of all the notable mountains in China, Yellow Mountain (Mt. Huangshan), to be found in the south of Anhui province, is probably the most famous. Originally known as Mt. Yishan it was renamed Mt. Huangshan in 747 A.D. in recognition of the legendary Huang Di, who was the reputed ancestor of the Chinese people and who made magic pills for immortality here.

Wu yue is the collective name given to China's most important mountains. It is said that you won't want to visit any other mountains after seeing wu yue but you won't wish to see even wu yue after returning from Yellow Mountain. This saying may give you some idea of the beauty and uniqueness of Yellow Mountain.

The strange pines, absurd stones, sea of clouds and hot springs are the four wonders of Yellow Mountain.

Etiquettes and Customs of China Major Tourist Source Countries and Regions

Unit 10

Topic Guidance

China Tourism Source Regions mainly include: Hong Kong, Macao & Taiwan; Asia and the Pacific; Europe and North America.

Different places have different etiquettes and customs, which reflect their unique culture.

The various etiquettes add to the enjoyment of our travel and it's important for the guide and tourists to understand different etiquettes and customs.

Warming-up

Read the following questions and discuss with your partner.

1. Which places have you visited? Can you illustrate some of their customs or etiquettes different from ours?
2. Which countries or regions have the most appealing customs or etiquettes to you?

Look at the following pictures and try to describe it in your own words.

Unit 10 Etiquettes and Customs of China Major Tourist Source Countries and Regions

Part A   Listening

Words List

etiquette	/ˈetiket/	n.	礼仪；礼节
ceremony	/ˈserəməni/	n.	仪式；礼节
represent	/ˌrepriˈzent/	v.	代表；象征
fold	/fəuld/	v.	折叠；合拢
gratitude	/ˈɡrætitjuːd/	n.	感激；感恩
courtesy	/ˈkəːtəsi/	n.	谦恭；礼貌
diligent	/ˈdilidʒənt/	adj.	勤勉的；用功的
punctual	/ˈpʌŋktʃuəl/	adj.	准时的；按时的
warmth	/wɔːmθ/	n.	温暖；热情
sincerity	/sinˈseriti/	n.	诚挚；真实
occasion	/əˈkeiʒn/	n.	场合；时机
fashionable	/ˈfæʃnəbl/	adj.	流行的；时髦的
relationship	/riˈleiʃnʃip/	n.	关系；关联
sever	/ˈsevə(r)/	v.	切断；分离
associate	/əˈsəuʃieit/	v.	使发生联系；使联合
funeral	/ˈfjuːnərəl/	n.	葬礼；出殡

Useful Expressions

show gratitude for sb.	对某人表示感谢
derive from	来源于
make a toast	敬酒
tend to	倾向于
get to the point	谈正题
be dressed in	穿着
be associated with	与……有关

Proper Nouns

kowtow ceremony	磕头礼仪
business suit	西装
cheongsam	旗袍

Activity 1: Spot dictation.

In Hong Kong, people (1)_____ when they meet. The handshake is rather (2)_____. When dinning, people knock the table top with (3)_____ to show their (4)_____ for others who pour the drink or tea for them. Such courtesy (5)_____

159

the "kowtow" ceremony. Don't turn a fish over at table, because it (6)_____a boat capsizing, and don't pour your own drink first. Instead, (7)_____about business or friendship.

In Hong Kong, Taiwan and Macao, people tend to be (8)_____.Before your conversation (9)_____, you can say some polite remarks and greetings with them to show your (10)_____.

Men wear (11)_____and women wear dress on(12)_____, and otherwise they dress informally with(13)_____, colorful and(14)_____clothes they like. In Taipei, it's popular for ladies to (15)_____beautiful cheongsam with their favorite (16)_____.

In these places, some gifts are (17)_____. For example, do not give Taiwanese scissors, knives or other cutting utensils as they traditionally indicate that you want to sever the (18)_____. Do not give (19)_____. handkerchiefs or straw sandals either, as they are associated with (20)_____.

Activity 2: Decide whether the following statements are True or False while listening to the paragraph again.

(   ) 1. People often offer a strong handshake upon meeting someone in Hong Kong.

(   ) 2. The practice of knocking the table top with folded fingers come from "kowtou" ceremony.

(   ) 3. People like to go town to the point directly in their conversation in Hong Kong, Taiwan, and Macao.

(   ) 4. People usually dress casually on informal occasions in Hong Kong, Taiwan, and Macao.

(   ) 5. Straw sandals can be given as a gift to Taiwanese.

Activity 3: Choose the correct answer while you are listening.

1. What do people in Hong Kong usually do when they meet foreigners?
    A. hug   B. kiss the cheek   C. handshake
2. Why don't Taiwanese like umbrella as a gift?
    A. It is not used often in their life.
    B. It has no indication.
    C. It has an inauspicious sound.
3. Which country has influenced Macao greatly?
    A. Spain   B. Portugal   C. Britain
4. Which place is not mentioned in the dialogue?
    A. Vitoria Peak B. Wan Chai   C. Stanley market
5. What do people in Macao eat when they drink tea?
    A. fruit   B. rice   C. dessert

Unit 10 Etiquettes and Customs of China Major Tourist Source Countries and Regions

Part B Speaking

Words List

itinerary	/aiˈtinərəri/	n.	旅程；旅行路线
bow	/baʊ/	v.	鞠躬；弯腰
ranking	/ˈræŋkiŋ/	n.	等级；地位
involved	/inˈvɔlvd/	adj.	相关的
deference	/ˈdefərəns/	n.	顺从；尊重
hierarchical	/ˌhaiəˈrɑːkikl/	adj.	分等级的
heel	/hiːl/	n.	脚后跟；踵
customary	/ˈkʌstəməri/	adj.	习惯的；惯例的
token	/ˈtəʊkən/	n.	纪念品
ostentetious	/ˌɔstenˈteiʃəs/	adj.	好夸耀的，炫耀的
wrap	/ræp/	v.	包装；卷
subtly	/ˈsʌtli/	adv.	敏锐地；精细地
gracious	/ˈgreiʃəs/	adj.	有礼的；得体的
chopstick	/ˈtʃɔpstik/	n.	筷子

Useful Expressions

keep pace with	与……同步
forms of speech	用语
social status	社会地位
business card	名片
depend on	依赖于
table manner	餐桌礼仪

Proper Nouns

cherry blossom	樱花
plum blossom	梅花
China Shandong International Travel Service	山东国旅

Situational dialogue 1

Miss Li Na, a guide from China Shandong International Travel Service in Jinan, is taking the tourists to Qingdao on bus, who will visit Korea and Japan by air from Qingdao Liu Ting Ariport.

T: tourists   G: guide

G: OK, Ladies and gentlemen, just now I've told you our travel itinerary and the matters we need to pay attention to. Are we clear now? If you have any other questions, ask me or call me, please. Let's take several minutes to learn about some etiquettes and customs in the two countries we will travel around, OK?

T: OK. Miss Li, their etiquettes are quite different from those in China, right?

G: Yes, one big difference is that Korean and Japanese usually bow when they meet and part from one another. The type of bow depends on the relationship and social or professional ranking of the people involved. And different forms of speech are used with elders to show deference and respect.

T: It seems that their youngsters show great respect to the elders.

G: That's right. They have similar traditional culture with us: To respect the elderly and take good care of the young. In fact, Korean culture is hierarchical and one's social status determines how one is treated. They have strict rules when meeting elders. Another difference is the way of sitting. As we often see in some Japanese and Korean films, people often sit on their heel no matter when they talk with friends or have meals and one point we must know is that you will be expected to remove your shoes upon entering many Japanese and Korean buildings, including homes. And when you are invited by a Japanese and Korean friend, it is customary to bring a small gift.

T: What gifts do they like?

G: A small token and not an ostentatious object is proper. For example, fruit or good quality chocolates or flowers are good choices if invited to a Korean's home, but gifts should be wrapped nicely. Use both hands when offering a gift and gifts are not opened when received. Korean like odd numbers and dislike the number 4. For Japanese, they are fond of pictures with cherry blossom, turtle, crane and pine, bamboo and plum blossom, and don't like the flower lotus, the animal fox, the colour green or purple, nor do they like number 4, 9 or 13. They dislike it that three persons are taken photos together.

T: Do they have some business rules?

G: Being punctual is very important and I know in Japan and korea, people use business cards a lot. You should receive a business card with both hands and bow subtly, yet graciously. Read the card with great interest. Simply taking the card and putting it in your pocket or wallet is considered rude.

T: Are there some table manners we need to know?

G: Usually, before the meals, Japanese will say: "Itadkimasu!", meaning "I gratefully receive", and after the meal, they will say: "Go-chiso-samadeshita!", meaning " thank you for the delicious meal". People can make sound when they eat food to show their appreciation. In Korea, however, do not make noises with spoon or chopsticks hitting the rice bowl or other food containers. When having a meal with the elderly, you have to wait for the elders to hold their spoon first and keep pace with them. Unlike people in China and Japan, during the meal, people should not hold the bowl of soup or rice.

Unit 10 Etiquettes and Customs of China Major Tourist Source Countries and Regions

T: I think their etiquettes are more complex than ours.

G: Haha, I believe we will learn more about their etiquettes during the travel.

Knowledge Improvement

Countries in Asia and the Pacific

Mainly including China, Japan, Korea, Philippines, Malaysia, Singapore, Indonesia, Thailand, Vietnam, Laos, Cambodia, Australia, and New Zealand and so on.

Some "dos and don'ts" in Singapore, Malaysia and Thailand

In Singapore, Malaysia, and Thailand, people consider head to be the home of the soul and thus head should not be touched. One shall never touch anything with their feet and while sitting cross-legged the sole of the foot shouldn't be pointed at. The feet in Thailand are considered spiritually as well as physically the lowest part of the body. Don't step over people's legs, even in a crowded place such as on a train; wait politely for them to move out of the way. Do not point things out or pick things up with your feet. And do not wave your feet around people's heads! If you accidentally touch someone with your foot, do apologize. People in Singapore, Malaysia, and Thailand, always use your right hand to eat food. Even if you're handling food with knife and fork, use their hand for eating. For taking or giving anything too, try to use your right hand. Apart from using right hand, always give properly wrapped gifts.

Activity 1: Group discussion.

All the students are divided into several groups to discuss what they have learned about the etiquettes and customs in Japan and Korea mentioned in the dialogue and combined with their experience. After discussion, each group choose a representative to make a presentation, and then the teacher should give the comment on students' answer.

Activity 2: Make up a dialogue.

Please practice the dialogue for 10 minutes with your deskmates. After that, the teacher names some students to choose a role to make up a dialogue and then gives comments on their performance if necessary.

Activity 3: Simulated guiding.

All the students are divided into several groups, and every group member may try to act as a local guide in class to simulate a situation of introducing some etiquettes and customs in a different country or region. Some phrases and expressions you have learnt may be used in your commentary.

Part C Reading

Words List

initial	/ɪˈnɪʃəl/	adj.	开始的；最初的
buddy-buddy	/ˈbʌdiˈbʌdi/	adj.	非常亲密的
back-slapping	/bækˈslæpɪŋ/	adj.	过分亲密的
grasp	/ɡrɑːsp/	v.	抓住；抓紧
release	/rɪˈliːs/	v.	松开；解开
academic	/ˌækəˈdemɪk/	adj.	教学的；学术的
violation	/ˌvaɪəˈleɪʃən/	n.	违反；违背
spouse	/spaʊs/	n.	配偶
generosity	/ˌdʒenəˈrɒsəti/	n.	慷慨；宽大
stupefy	/ˈstjuːpɪfaɪ/	v.	使惊奇；惊讶
sumptuous	/ˈsʌmptʃuəs/	adj.	奢侈的；华丽的
proffer	/ˈprɒfə(r)/	v.	提供
gambit	/ˈɡæmbɪt/	n.	话题；开始
offensive	/əˈfensɪv/	adj.	讨厌的；无礼的
option	/ˈɒpʃən/	n.	选择
affable	/ˈæfəbl/	adj.	和蔼可亲的
hospitable	/hɒˈspɪtəbl/	adj.	好客的；招待周到的
racism	/ˈreɪsɪzəm/	n.	种族主义；种族歧视
abortion	/əˈbɔːʃn/	n.	流产；堕胎
sensitive	/ˈsensətɪv/	adj.	敏感的；灵敏的
criticism	/ˈkrɪtɪsɪzəm/	n.	批评；批判
divulge	/daɪˈvʌldʒ/	v.	泄露；暴露
affiliation	/əˌfɪliˈeɪʃən/	n.	联系，关系
decline	/dɪˈklaɪn/	v.	拒绝
whistle	/ˈwɪsl/	v.	吹口哨
scratch	/skrætʃ/	v.	抓；挠
nefarious	/nɪˈfeəriəs/	adj.	邪恶的；穷凶极恶的
pemissible	/pəˈmɪsəbl/	adj.	可允许的
insult	/ˈɪnsʌlt/	v.	侮辱；凌辱
inappropriate	/ˌɪnəˈprəʊpriət/	adj.	不适当的；不相称的

Unit 10 Etiquettes and Customs of China Major Tourist Source Countries and Regions

Useful Expressions

extend one's hand	伸出手
be reserved for	供……之用
watch out	注意，留神
out of place	不合适
be set-aside for	为……保留
be obliged to do	不得不
RSVP (=Reply, if you please.)	请回复
make a commitment	做出承诺
bend over	俯身，弯腰
urge sb. to do	督促某人去做
body contact	身体接触
thumbs-up	竖起大拇指
table napkin	餐巾纸

Proper Nouns

Thank-you letter	感谢信

Etiquettes and Customs in Europe and North America

Europe

Handshakes

Handshakes are standard business greeting gestures throughout Europe. However, the European handshake is usually exchanged before and after every meeting, no matter how many meetings you've already had. An exception is Great Britain, where, as in the United States, an initial handshake is often the only one you'll receive.

European Handshakes are more formal and less buddy-buddy than those in the United States. You will not find a lot of back-slapping at handshaking time. A quick grasp and release is the norm. In most European countries, handshakes are firm. An exception is France, where a lighter grasp is customary. Finally, it's customary to let women and those in a higher rank to extend their hands first in Europe.

Names and Titles

It's unusual in Europe for people to use first names immediately. Wait until he asks you to call him by his first name or uses a familiar form of address with you. Titles, especially academic titles, are always used in Europe. In the United States, it's unusual for a Professor to be called *Doctor* or *Professor* outside of the classroom, but in European countries, professors, along with lawyers, medical doctors, and others are introduced with their title(s).

Dining and Entertaining

Europeans don't do business breakfasts. In France, Austria, Germany, Great Britain, The Netherlands, Norway, Denmark, Sweden, Finland, Portugal, and Spain, talking business over lunch is not a violation of etiquette. In the Czech Republic, Italy, and Greece, on the other hand, you do not talk business over lunch unless your host initiates it.

Dinner in Europe is usually reserved for social entertaining. Depending on the country, you may start dinner as early as 6:30 p.m. or as late as 11:00 p.m. Depending on the country your spouse may be invited.

Dining is taken seriously in most of Europe as an expression of generosity. In some countries, such as Italy and Greece, this generosity can reach stupefying levels; it can be virtually impossible to pick up a check in Italy and virtually impossible not to overeat or overdrink in Greece. But it's rude to refuse dinner invitations or any of the sumptuous items proffered to you at a dinner.

Here are some general dining rules.

(1) In Norway, Sweden, Finland, Denmark, be on time for dinner. Elsewhere, being fashionably late is acceptable.

(2) No host gift is expected in Great Britain.

(3) Do not take wine to a dinner in the Netherlands, France, or Belgium. It insinuates that you think the host's cellar is lacking.

Social Taboos

In many European countries, asking people what they do or asking them a personal question as an opening conversational gambit is a serious mistake. Europeans are, for the most part, more formal and reserved about such matters than Americans are.

Watch out for these gesture-related mistakes.

(1) The American gesture for "OK" using a circle formed by forefinger and thumb is offensive in Germany.

(2) Showing your palm to someone is offensive in Greece.

(3) Keeping your hands in your pockets is rude.

(4) Back-slapping is out of place in northern Europe.

(5) Having your hands below the table while dining in France, Germany, and Austria is rude.

North America

Greetings

In North America, greetings are offered in the form of a hand shake, a hug, or a kiss on the cheek as dictated by the relationship's social distance and the comfort level of the parties involved. The rule for the "American Handshake" is a firm handshake: not too soft and not too hard. Shake a couple of times. You should stand and not sit when giving or receiving a

Unit 10 Etiquettes and Customs of China Major Tourist Source Countries and Regions

handshake. Like the British, Canadians are thought to be quite modest and reserved when making introductions for the first time. When meeting, a firm handshake is the best option. Try to avoid being overly familiar and making too much body contact, such as hugging or back slapping. This is usually set-aside for close friends and family. Generally you will find that most Canadians are very affable, polite and hospitable.

Conversation

People in North America tend to speak in a direct informal manner. They are usually polite and friendly. Conversation topics to avoid include politics, religion, homosexuality, racism, abortion, and criticism of the government. It's best to have a strong relationship in place before speaking about sensitive topics. Americans do not usually divulge how much money they make or how much they paid for certain things like a houses, car, etc. It tends to be considered rude to ask and is even more uncomfortable to discuss. It is considered impolite in social and professional settings, especially when first meeting someone, to ask if they are married or dating; their political or religious affiliations or beliefs; or their age, weight, race or other personal physical matters. Personal matters should not be brought up except to those with whom one is highly familiar. Americans and Canadians value their personal space and tend to be comfortable with 2~3 feet of personal space during conversations. For most of them there is little to no touching during conversations. This may be different between good friends and family. They value direct eye contact during conversations. It is viewed as a sign of respect and interest in what the person speaking is saying. Staring is considered rude and to be avoided.

Invitation and Appointment

When receiving an invitation, one is obliged to respond in kind as soon as possible. This means if receiving the invitation by phone, reply by phone, etc.. One must accept or decline even if "RSVP" is not specified. Accepting an invitation is making a commitment. If one cannot be sure if the obligation can be kept, the invitation should be declined. "Thank You" letters may be offered for any situation. A thank you letter is not required for all situations, but is never incorrect if sincere.

Table manners are important in America. In general Americans try to eat neatly, without making a lot of noise. If something on the table is out of their reach, they politely ask someone to pass it to them. Food should be lifted up to the mouth. Do not bend over to eat it. Sit up as straight as you can without being uncomfortable. Do not talk with your mouth full. Table napkins are placed on your lap, folded in half if they are very large. If you are in a small group, it is polite to wait to start eating until the host sits down and begins. With larger groups, you may begin after noting that a few people have begun. You may also begin if the host urges you to.

Be on time for appointments since punctuality is important in the American culture. Americans value punctuality and expect things to be on time. This includes appointments, services, and deliveries. It is best to show up exactly on time for appointments and social functions.

Gestures

The OK sign and "thumbs up" sign mean good or acceptable and are commonly used throughout the country.

Whistling at performance events is a sign of appreciation. Waving can indicate both greeting and saying goodbye and is usually done by moving the entire hand from left to right with the palm facing outward.

Raising the middle finger is seen as highly offensive. Avoid using it, even when pointing to objects or scratching your face.

Pointing is considered rude in the west, and therefore one should not point in public as it may not be clear if one is pointing to another person. If it is clear one is pointing to an object or nefarious lass, the gesture is acceptable.

Spitting is usually unacceptable in public settings. If you have to spit, it's best to use a tissue and then throw it away.

In many French-speaking areas of Canada, it is considered to rude to eat while walking on the street. Avoid referring to Canadians as Americans.

Tipping

Many restaurant servers in the US and Canada receive the majority of their income from tips and the customary gratuity is between 15% and 20% of the non-tax total of the bill. If one receives very poor food service, it is best to speak to manager so that the problem may be resolved. It is permissible in an extreme situation not to tip. Insulting the waiter by leaving a penny on the table as the "tip" is inappropriate.

Activity 1: Choose the correct answer to complete the following sentences.

1. In Europe, it's polite to let women and_____to extend their hands first.
   A. your fellows   B. those in low rank   C. people who are superior to you
2. In Europe, asking people_____as an opening conversational topic is not inappropriate.
   A. their age   B. their earnings   C. the time
3. The rule for_____handshake is a firm handshake: not too soft and not too hard.
   A. American   B. Europeans   C. Britains
4. Americans and Canadians value their personal space and tend to be comfortable with _____of personal space during conversations.
   A. 1 feet   B. 2~3 feet   C. 5 feet
5. Raising the middle finger in North America is seen as_____.
   A. merry   B. affable   C. disgusting

Activity 2: Fill in the blanks according to what you have learnt.

1._____ are standard business greeting gestures throughout Europe.

Unit 10 Etiquettes and Customs of China Major Tourist Source Countries and Regions

2. Dining is taken seriously in most of Europe as_____.

3. People in North America tend to speak in a direct informal manner. They are usually _____.

4. Whistling at performance events is_____.

5. Many restaurant servers in the US and Canada receive the majority of their income from_____.

Activity 3: Answer the following open questions in brief.

1. What are the rules of handshake in Europe?
2. What are the dinner rules mentioned in the passage in Europe?
3. What are the topics to avoid in North America?
4. What are the table manners in America?
5. How much do North American usually give tips when dining in the restaurant?

Part D   Writing

Compose a Summary Report
撰写带团总结

带团总结是导游带完一次旅游团的自我总结，是必要的后续性工作，通过带团总结，导游员可以看出取得了哪些成绩，存在哪些缺点和不足，不断积累经验；管理者可以看出这条线路走得如何、是否具有更大的推荐价值。撰写带团总结，导游员需要结合客人的反馈信息，了解各项活动是否基本上按照行程中的规定开展，与预先估计的是否一致。具体来说，应包括以下内容。

（1）成绩和缺点。将带团中的经验和教训进行分析、研究、概括、集中，并上升到理论的高度来认识。

（2）今后的计划。提出今后的工作任务和要求，吸取这次带团工作的经验和教训，明确努力方向，提出改进措施等。

在撰写带团总结过程中，同时要注意做到以下几点。

（1）带团小结必须客观、真实。

（2）高度概括。在记述全面的同时，突出中心，记述带团过程中有意义的内容，语言简练，言简意赅。

（3）针对不同产品，重点不同。不同旅游产品的带团小结也应有所区别。比如，红色旅游团队的带团小结应突出旅游景点的革命和教育意义、游客的感受和导游自身的想法等，观光旅游团队的带团小结则应侧重于不同景点的观赏价值以及游客对景点的欢迎程度、评价等。

Sample

Situation: Xiao Wu is a tour guide from Wuhan International Travel Service. He just got his first chance to serve two foreign guests. The following is his work summary.

Summary Report

Today it's my first time to take foreigners to travel as a guide. The task was very simple: To meet an old couple named Eire in the dock and then to take them to visit Wuhan and at last to see them off at the airport.

At first, I was told the couple was from England, so I prepared some topics about London, but after I met them, I knew they came from Ireland. My mind went blank. Fortunately, I knew a lot about Wuhan. Thus, I began to introduce Wuhan to them. The couple was very nice. Although my English was not fluent, they still showed great interest in my introduction. Afterwards, I took them to have meals and then visited the city, and took them to the airport.

When we got to the airport, we learned that the plane was delayed. So I waited together with them for about one hour, and then helped them to check the luggage and prepare other procedures. At last, everything was ready. My patience and good service won their appreciation. One embarrassing matter was that I forgot the English term "Exit", thus I had a lot of difficulty in making them understand me. Before they left, they gave me an envelope in which I found 100 yuan. That was the tip for me!

All in all, what is very important for a successful guide is to make enough preparation and try to be calm and patient when having trouble. Learning necessary English service terms is also important when your guests are foreigners.

Simulated Writing

Directions: Li Yan is a new tour guide. Please use the following reference to write a summary report for her.

尽管这是第一次独立带团，团运行得很顺畅。因为团很小，仅 13 人，也很轻松。整个运作过程都是按照行程安排进行的，无任何偏差。这次的经历很令人难忘。

游览和食宿：景点、住宿和餐饮的安排十分妥当。客人对湖南和湖南菜赞不绝口。

司机和车辆：王师傅经验丰富，热心助人。当我因为处理一些事情无法及时回答客人的问题时，他便帮我向客人解释或回答客人常问的一些问题。正是由于有了他的帮助，我的工作得以顺利开展。另外，车内设施良好。

客人反馈：导游李燕的知识并不够丰富，经验有待提高，但她热情周到、认真细致、工作负责、开朗幽默，还是很受欢迎的，跟她相处很愉快。为了营造开心和舒适的氛围，导游李燕付出了辛勤的劳动，使大家对此次旅游活动很满意，湖南的山水景象令人印象深刻。

概况：初次出团让我了解了实际操作一个团队的关键所在，这对一个新导游来说是相当重要的。我很高兴能有机会带这次的美国学生团队。本人也深感荣幸能够在讲

Unit 10 Etiquettes and Customs of China Major Tourist Source Countries and Regions

解、回答客人提问、解决问题、做出决定等方面展示一些带团必备的技能。尤其重要的是，我的努力得到了客人的认可。希望在今后的工作中继续努力，迎接挑战，经受考验。

对我而言，学会带团是很重要的。特此感谢我的指导老师和部门经理，没有他们，这次的工作就不会完成得这么顺利。在此还要感谢友谊旅行社，感谢贵公司为我提供了这次宝贵的机会。

Part E Practical Training

Training item 1: Oral Presentation

Directions: You are required to work with your group members to finish the task in this part. Every group should choose a country or a region and give an introduction of the customs and etiquettes there. After preparation and practice, a group member will be asked to make an oral presentation, other students may have additional remarks or explanation if necessary. And then teacher gives comments on students' performance.

Training item 2: Role-play

Directions: All the students in the class are divided into several groups, every member in the group choose one role to perform. Students should use the language they have learnt as far as possible.

Situation 1: Mr. Green, a tourist from USA, plans to visit Hong Kong and Macao next day. He is inquiring about some customs and etiquettes from Chinese guide Lily.

Situation 2: The Chinese tour guide Lily is going to take several tourists from Europe to take part in a dinner party in Japan. Lily is giving her brief introduction of the dinner etiquettes in Japan.

Situation 3: The Chinese tour guide Kelly is going to take several Chinese tourists to America. Before she goes abroad, she must grasp the points for attention about the etiquettes and customs of North America. Now she is discussing some problems about etiquettes and customs with her colleagues.

Training item 3: Outside-class Work

Directions: Please find more knowledge about customs and etiquettes about China tourism source countries from books, Internet or some other channels. Try to compare and explain some characteristics of them and then make a brief introduction.

Knowledge links

Mid-Autumn Festival in Different Countries

China's Mid-Autumn Festival is traditionally celebrated on the fifteenth day of the eighth lunisolar month. The festival is the second most important festival after the Spring Festival to Chinese people. Every year, when the festival comes, people go home from every corner of the country and the world to meet their family and have dinner with them.

Mid-Autumn Festival in Japan

The Mid-Autumn Festival is named Tsukimi or Otsukimi (literally means moon-viewing) in Japan. Celebrations of the festival take place on the 15th day of the eighth month of the traditional Japanese Lunisor calendar (usually takes place in September of the solar calendar).

The Tsukimi custom or moon-viewing custom originated from the Chinese Mid-Autumn Festival. Custom of viewing the moon and holding festival parties appeared over 1000 years ago when tradition of the Chinese Mid-Autumn Festival was introduced to Japan.

Unlike the Chinese, who eat moon cakes to celebrate the festival, the Japanese usually eat rice dumplings called Tsukimi dango. The tradition is now so popular in Japan that some people repeat the activities for several evenings following the appearance of the full moon during the eighth lunisolar month.

Mid-Autumn Festival in Vietnam

The Mid-Autumn festival is named "Tết Trung Thu" in Vietnamese. The main celebration is displaying flower lanterns. During the festival, there are flower lanterns displays across the country. Competitions of flower lanterns design are held and the winner will be rewarded. In some places, lion dances are arranged in the evenings of 14th and 15th of the eighth month.

The dances are performed by both non-professional children group and trained professional groups. Lion dance groups go to houses asking for permission to perform for them. If accepted by the host, they will perform as a wish of luck and good fortune. The host gives back lucky money in return. Unlike the Chinese moon cakes in round shape, moon cakes in Vietnam are typically square.

Mid-Autumn Festival in Singapore

As a country with most of the people being the Chinese, Singapore has long been the place where the Mid-Autumn Day is attached importance to. It is the time for them to greet each other and express their gratitude. As friends, relatives or business partners, they send moon cakes to each other to express their gracious greetings and good wishes.

Singapore is a tourist country. Mid-Autumn Day is a good chance to attract tourists. Whenever the Mid-Autumn Day is approaching, the renowned tourist areas including Wujie Road, Singapore Riverside, the Chinatown and the Chinese Garden are redecorated gaily. When the night falls gradually, the red lanterns come on, lightening the streets and lanes and filling them with the celebratory and festival atmosphere.

A giant dragon lantern was erected on the Singapore Riverside to celebrate the festival last year. The giant lantern, which was 300 meters (990 feet) long and 4.5 meters (14.85 feet) high, costing 70000 USD. When the night came, the whole giant dragon lantern shined, tinting the river aglow. What a tremendous spectacle! In the China Town, there was not only the jumbo lantern imported from the countries including Nepal and Vietnam, but also 44 little delicate dragons composed by 1364 small red lanterns. All of them made the China Town even more attractive. A large-scaled dreamlike fancy lantern carnival was held at the Imperial Garden, a landscape garden with the style of the ancient Chinese garden. The popular Disney lanterns as well as the giant lanterns in the shapes of the Temple of Heaven in Beijing and the dragon particularly caught people's attention.

Mid-Autumn Festival in the South Korea

The Mid-Autumn Day is also named "qiu xi". It is also a tradition of Korean to present gifts to relatives and friends on this festival. Therefore, it is named "Thanksgiving Day" as well. On their holiday table, the festival is marked as "Thanksgiving Day" in English. The Mid-Autumn is a general festival in Korea, and there would be a three days' holiday. During these days, they would come back to their hometown to visit their relatives. Thus, it is the season for sale one month before the festival. The major companies would give big discounts to attract people to give gifts to each other. On this day, Korean would have a kind of traditional snack, which resembles the Chinese dumpling.

参 考 文 献

[1] 纪春，裴松青. 英语导游教程 [M]. 2版. 北京：旅游教育出版社，2008.
[2] 朱华. 英语导游实务教程[M]. 北京：北京大学出版社，2009.
[3] 朱华. 导游英语[M]. 北京：高等教育出版社，2007.
[4] 李云川. 缤纷中国[M]. 大连：大连理工大学出版社，2008.
[5] 刘泓，浩瀚. 用英语说中国风俗民情[M]. 北京：科学技术文献出版社，2009.
[6] 庞规荃. 中国旅游地理[M]. 2版. 北京：旅游教育出版社，2009.
[7] 丁树德. 实用旅游英语口语教程[M]. 天津：天津大学出版社，2006.
[8] 关肇远. 导游英语口语[M]. 北京：高等教育出版社，2008.
[9] 梁文生. 导游基础知识[M]. 济南：山东科学技术出版社，2009.
[10] 陆志宝. 导游英语[M]. 北京：旅游教育出版社，2003.
[11] 程丛喜，Lynn Fair. 导游英语阅读[M]. 武汉：武汉大学出版社，2007.
[12] 潘惠霞. 旅游英语[M]. 北京：旅游教育出版社，2004.
[13] 赵宝国. 21世纪实用旅游英语教程. [M]. 上海：学林出版社，2005.
[14] 段开成，黄宝琴. 旅游英语[M]. 天津：南开大学出版社，2008.
[15] 赵德芳. 休闲旅游英语教程[M]. 上海：上海人民出版社，2003.
[16] 王兴斌. 中国旅游客源概况[M]. 北京：旅游教育出版社，1996.
[17] 张靖. 英语导游基础教程[M]. 北京：清华大学出版社，2009.
[18] 王向宁. 实用导游英语[M]. 北京：北京大学出版社，2010.
[19] 袁祖文. 北京英语导游[M]. 北京：旅游教育出版社，1999.
[20] 刘飞，李凯平. 用英语说中国[M]. 上海：上海科学普及出版社，2008.
[21] 导游资格考试辅导编写组. 导游基础知识[M]. 济南：山东科学技术出版社，2009.
[22] Robert W.McIntosh.Tourism Principles, Practices, Philosophies [M]. New York: John Wiley& Sons, Inc,1995.
[23] Zhang Qizhi.Traditional Chinese Culture [M].Beijing: Foreign Language Press, 2008.
[24] http://en.wikipedia.org/wiki/Etiquette
[25] http://www1.chinaculture.org/library/2008-02/07/content_23319.htm
[26] http://www.paulnoll.com/China/Minorities/index.html
[27] http://www.travelchinaguide.com/intro/nationality/
[28] http://www.chinavista.com/entravel/culture.php
[29] http://www.warriortours.com/intro/cuisine_culture.htm
[30] http://chinese.chnedu.com/web/aboutchina/catesworld/drugdish/index.htm
[31] http://xiangge.lila2009.blog.163.com/blog/static/7348245220090234546880/
[32] http://www.tasly.com/show.aspx?id=3225&cid=33
[33] http://chinese.chnedu.com/web/aboutchina/catesworld/dishfaction/lu.htm